# HEALING THE RIFT:

## BRIDGING THE GAP BETWEEN SCIENCE AND SPIRITUALITY

BY
LEO KIM, PH.D.

CAMBRIGE HOUSE PRESS

NEW YORK § TORONTO

Published by
Cambridge House Press
New York, NY 10001
www.camhousepress.com

Library of Congress Cataloging-in-Publication Data

Kim, Leo, 1942-
    Healing the rift : bridging the gap between science and spirituality / by
Leo Kim.
        p. cm.
    Includes bibliographical references.
    ISBN 978-0-9787213-2-9 (paperback : alk. paper)
    1. Religion and science. 2. Spirituality. I. Title.

BL240.3K548 2008
215--dc22

                                        2008009484
10 9 8 7 6 5 4 3 2 1

Printed in the United States of America.

*To the Kim family whose three generations of struggle
has led to a better life for their descendants*

# Contents

# PREFACE

*Science is not only compatible with spirituality; it is a profound source of spirituality.*

–Carl Sagan

Water and waves. I have always found ripples on water to be mesmerizing. By age five the arrival of a wave could magically transform me into a white coat-clad scientist, swirling a flask of bubbling green elixir. In the laboratory, my mother beamed, her delighted gaze meeting mine. In that instant, I knew she shared my dream, and I needed no further encouragement. I don't know if it was the next wave or the hundredth that dissolved my daydream.

My passion resembled hunger and thirst, my hunger briefly satisfied by a library card and my thirst quenched by experimentation. I saved my modest earnings and anxiously awaited the mail, which brought ingredients for my alchemy. On any given day, the neighbors might catch a whiff of spent gunpowder, behold a mushroom cloud hovering over a demolished anthill, or cringe after a window-rattling explosion.

I graduated to rockets as evidenced by charred shingles, a wet roof, and a tangled garden hose. I did not know that, sooner or later, life resembles an out-of-control rocket, often with tragic results. Although he did not share my love of pyrotechnics, Stanley was my best friend. The last time I saw him, we both wore our new Cub Scout uniforms. Stanley, however, occupied a coffin.

Stanley's parents sat huddled in the front row. His mother wiped her eyes with a handkerchief. His father stared ahead, dead-eyed.

Stanley was an only child. In the Central Valley of California summer sizzled, but everyone wore black except for a few Cubs clad in their uniforms. Floral arrangements provided the only color in the church. The church's silence, the images before me, and the sweet floral fragrance contributed to my trancelike state. The minister spoke softly as he said, "Sometimes, we cannot understand God's will. Stanley is in heaven."

I was too shocked by my friend's death to contemplate this notion, although I could see Stanley's body in his casket.

The gentle voice of the minister stilled, and people shuffled forward to comfort Stanley's parents. The sounds of grief echoed through the church. After a while, several adults took up the coffin, and a few of Stanley's fellow Cubs followed the procession out of the church. Stanley and his uncle, a crop duster, had died in a plane crash after hitting a power line. A few days earlier, Stanley had invited me to join them on this plane ride. He ran over to my shanty-like house, explaining in his excitement that we would fly over the fields where I worked. My heart raced with equal excitement, but I needed permission from my mother, who fussed over everything. She said it was too dangerous. My father, who always worried about money, insisted that I had to work. Sometimes, one of them would take my side. This time, however, both refused to reconsider.

After learning of the crash, I felt too numb to cry. I also recalled thinking that I, too, could have been in a coffin.

I hid my grief and trauma. Just as each Cub Scout badge I earned was put away in a cigar box, nearly all of my childhood memories, along with my sense of loss over Stanley, were placed in a mental cigar box. I focused on my dream of becoming a scientist. Ultimately, I became a physical organic chemist, and I had no occasion to ponder death or spiritual matters until decades later when another death occurred.

When death again grabbed my attention, I questioned what had happened to Stanley and to all those who die. I reopened the box that hid my childhood memories, thus beginning a 25-year process of questioning the nature of our existence. My work involved biology and chemistry, but my quest to understand human existence also led to an expanded study of cosmology and physics. I tackled the big questions: Where did we come from? How did life originate? What is reality? How can mind and consciousness emerge from brain and body? I realized that science doesn't have the answers to these questions—only suppositions.

Although I was baptized as a Christian, I dealt with religion and spirituality as an agnostic while devoutly kneeling at science's altar. I pondered these questions, and spirituality began to inch back into my life. Beginning as a distant whisper, the voice grew nearer. The image of spirituality changed into a welcome friend who cherished our world. I found a fascinating contrast between science and spirituality and, in the contrast, I also found unexpected harmony.

Science attempts to explain our world without a creator, spirit, or design, and constantly seeks new information from which to revise its theories. Spirituality accepts that the most important aspects of our world are hidden and beyond human comprehension, and it identifies this realm as composed of the spirit, the soul, and God. Are we simply a collection of cells in a human body that eventually becomes ill and perishes when it fails? Many scientists support this theory, while spiritual beliefs contradict it.

Is there a plan for us? Science explains our bodies as mechanisms of the material realm, ignoring the issue of any possible plan or design. Spirituality, on the other hand, views our bodies as both material and immaterial, asserting that there is a "plan."

Most of us would like to believe there is a plan for us, which would endow our brief time on Earth with some higher meaning. Although many scientists are spiritual people, many feel their spirituality slipping away. Their scientific discoveries about our world seem to diminish or negate the possibility of something greater. I, too, was skeptical of spiritual concepts. But I realized that, if I intended to embark upon this quest to understand human existence, I couldn't reject out of hand the accumulated wisdom and beliefs of thousands of years. I felt compelled to scrutinize both spiritual beliefs and scientific discoveries in order to determine if a new truth would emerge.

I discovered that science in no way diminished or negated the possibility of something greater. Although science is based on facts, it does not explain our beginnings and existence. In seeking answers to these questions, I discovered extraordinary scientific theories that appear to be faith-based. As a result, I could no longer avoid confronting the spiritual dimension.

These questions are also the focus of philosophy, religion, and spirituality. I've organized this book around these questions: our origins, our reality, and the emergence of mind from body and brain, culminating in my views of science and spirituality by utilizing 21st-century scientific concepts of our existence and reality.

Yet much of science is based on a 19th-century worldview. Since then, scientists have embraced materialism—the belief that all reality is physical. Materialism is a primary cause for the rift between science and spirituality.

With the exception of physicists, scientists typically regard matter as being composed of billiard ball-like component atoms. This materialistic perspective leads to several conclusions which are incompatible with spiritual beliefs. The first conclusion by materialists is that reality is simply physical and that spirit, or immaterial essence, is myth. The second is that the mind and consciousness are merely the result of brain activities. These assumptions logically eliminate free will, since if all the workings of the universe and humans are mechanical, as many scientists posit, humans cannot influence the future. Finally, the third is that since we are but matter, when we die nothing survives—neither mind nor spirit.

But what is life? And what really happens after death? Whether a person lives seven years or 70, is life merely a succession of vignettes of memories, feelings, and experiences that vanish when we die? Is that it—like they never happened at all? Seeking alternatives to the materialistic perspective, I searched for scientific evidence for existence after death. Perhaps, I reasoned, many people embrace spirituality in the hope of an afterlife.

Spiritual and religious teachings posit spirit, soul, afterlife, and God. So, can we even hope to resolve the conflicts of science and spirituality?

The reductionist approach has been highly successful for scientists. Reductionists believe that scientific explanations are inherently produced by the analysis of lower-level components. Thus, if a scientist seeks to understand a living organism, he must first understand organs, then tissues, then cells, then molecular, and before cellular components. This approach enables scientists to build upon prior discoveries.

However, biological scientists have not gone to the most fundamental level of our world in order to understand human beings. I deliberately followed new scientific discoveries down to the most basic units of existence—string-like waves. But the waves that make up our reality are as illusive as the theories which might describe them. And these waves only exist in the presence of consciousness, vanishing when not observed. Incredibly, between the waves is space which holds deeper, darker mysteries.

Science is a disciplined belief system. It is designed to utilize specific methods of tests and verifications to understand our world. Since both science and spirituality are belief systems, the teachings of each can be used to illuminate the other, with the ultimate goal of discovering the truth about life and what our world is all about.

My journey took me on a tour of the mind-boggling scientific concepts of the creation of the universe, life, and humankind. New theories reveal a startling view of reality. Recent breakthroughs explain how mind and consciousness emerge from body and brain, overturning previous dogmas and offering new healing methods. New studies provide fascinating insights into the possibility of an afterlife. Comparing 21st-century science with spiritual beliefs, I found that a new truth was emerging. I realized that water and waves were apt metaphors for my life and our reality. Like water finding its own level, I discovered how the rift between science and spirituality can be healed.

I invite you now to take this journey with me. Together, let's discover what's between the waves that make up our world and where our potential lies.

> *There are only two ways to live your life;*
> *One is as though nothing is a miracle.*
> *The other is as if everything is.*
> *I believe in the latter.*

> –Albert Einstein

# WHERE DID WE COME FROM?

# 1
# CREATION

*[We need] a deep mystical awakening the likes of which the planet has never witnessed before—a mystical awakening that is truly planetary.*

–Matthew Fox

The dice were rolling—survival or death. In the early 1980s, 10 West at UCLA was the second largest bone marrow transplantation unit in the world. But the dice were loaded. The odds for patient survival were low, only about one in four.

At this and other cancer centers, I observed many bald, emaciated cancer patients with eyes that revealed fear of their fate. Their weakened bodies and forced smiles broke any onlooker's heart. Mine was no exception.

One young patient at the outset of the program stood out. With her blond hair and bubbly demeanor, she could have easily been mistaken for a student, an unlikely patient in the hospital. Talking to other patients, gesturing to punctuate words, her voice full of enthusiasm and passion, Doris smiled at everyone as she came over to meet me. Our introduction was brief. She asked me about new drugs for cancer and leukemia. Her alert gaze and forward leaning posture seemed to shout, "Tell me more—I want to know everything!"

Her intense green eyes impressed me most. They seemed to peer into my soul and expressed such innocence, as though pleading, "Please give me hope."

As I continued with the tour of 10 West, an unfamiliar feeling grew inside me. I believed that Doris would survive. Why? She was so animated and vibrant. I didn't want to think about how she would look after high-dose chemotherapy and the loss of her hair.

For many leukemia patients, bone marrow transplantation provides their only hope for survival. Many of the patients at 10 West were young and at different stages in this rescue effort. After chemotherapy, they received radiation treatment—the equivalent of being a mile or so from the epicenter of the Hiroshima atomic blast. Side effects included fatigue, nausea, vomiting, diarrhea, mouth sores, skin problems, loss of appetite, and depression.

My thoughts drifted to those who would not survive—for them, death existed. A host of potential dangers also existed for these patients—failure of the chemotherapy, graft immune-cell attacks on their fragile bodies, viral and bacterial infections, organ failure, drug reactions, or the complications arising from an imperfect donor match. At this and all of the cancer centers I visited, I learned the grim statistics of survival. But the patients were not statistics. I always felt shaken for several days after these visits.

THE SEARCH

Dr. Robert Peter Gale allowed me to see 10 West, his staff, and some of his patients located on the top floor of the hospital overlooking Santa Monica, California. As I gazed outside, students laughed and read on the lawn, oblivious to the imminence of death.

As the research and development director for a multinational company in charge of their biomedical efforts, I evaluated the use of interferon and other new wonder drugs that employed the body's immune-defense systems. I wanted to know how a procedure such as bone marrow transplantation compared to conventional chemical-drug approaches, as well as the new biotechnology drugs, in treating cancer. I had visited several top cancer clinics that utilized various drugs to treat the disease. These tours initiated a change in me from a confident, often cocky scientist to a confused individual seeking an answer to our existence, purpose, and future.

My feelings of helplessness as I witnessed people die of cancer became a defining event in my life. As you already realize, cancer patents suffer from extreme pain, not simply physical weakness due to the wasting away of their bodies.

Several years passed before I realized that the tour of this cancer ward became the catalyst of my quest to study spiritual methods of healing. Little did I know, when I visited 10 West at UCLA, that these clinical events, my technical and scientific endeavors, and my own spiritual pursuit would converge and prompt me to investigate an ageless mystery.

I asked: Where did we come from? In my search for the answer to this question, I realized how little we understood our human origins. As in the quotation from Matthew Fox that began this chapter, I yearned for a deep mystical awakening. So many of us do. There had to be a means by which to reconcile science and spirituality that would catalyze my spiritual awakening. Both disciplines address where we came from, but can recent scientific beliefs of our beginnings be consistent with spirituality?

UPIXELS

In the 1990s, during an airplane trip in which I sat scrunched in a middle seat, I heard two men discussing their computer business. I put down my book and tried to nap. When the conversation of the two, who were seated behind me switched to science, I perked up. They said that most modern concepts of science such as String Theory were mystifying.

Without the impossible feat of twisting my body to face them, I mentally formulated a computer analogy as a response. Pixels on a computer screen are the smallest pieces of the image. In other words, it is the combination of pixels that allows us to see these images. Similarly, we could think of our reality as arising from pixel-like entities. I coined the term "upixels" to represent universal pixels. These upixels are a billion trillion times smaller than subatomic matter. They somehow become energy, matter, motion, time, gravity, and our reality.

So, if upixels are the fundamental ingredients that form everything in the universe, where did they come from? Hence, where did we come from? I could have told the two men behind me that scientists are attempting to understand what upixels are, where they come from, and what rules transform them to everything we experience, but I did not. Instead, I pondered and investigated these pieces of the universe.

The theories that attempt to explain upixels will be described later in a discussion of reality in Chapter 4. No uniform name denotes these. Scientists use jargon such as strings, quarks, leptons, and other technical terms. Because we do not know the basic unit of everything, I decided to arbitrarily use the term upixels. Scientists believe that upixels are some form of energy that cannot be adequately described. I find this assertion most interesting, since Eastern traditions have taught for thousands of years that everything is energy.

For now, it is important to keep the upixels in mind, because they aid me in explaining our origins, our nature, and reality itself.

### THE RIDDLE OF CREATION: WAS THERE A BEGINNING?

The question of creation is a major point of conflict between science and certain religions. Scientists attempt to explain the beginning of the universe without resorting to a Divine Being or the idea of intelligent design. I will contrast science's perspective with spiritual and religious teaching later in the book. For now, I want to address science's perspective.

The first of many mysteries of creation is how upixels became our world and reality. In the early 20th century, cosmologists discovered that the universe is expanding. Armed with powerful new telescopes that allowed a view into distant space, astronomers found that stars and galaxies were moving away from us. The distant galaxies whizzed away from us at speeds approaching that of light. Why was this happening?

Before this discovery, Einstein and other scientists thought the universe was static and there was no shrinkage or expansion of it—not that all distant galaxies were flying away from us. After this discovery, however, the universe was believed to have started with an enormous explosion. Prior to this explosion, all of the upixels were compressed into a dot-sized space. In the instant before our universe was born only upixels existed. Nothing else. For a totally unknown reason, this dot suddenly exploded outward with enormous force and speed in an event called the Big Bang.

## THE BIG BANG

This explosion was the most powerful that the universe has ever produced, with a temperature millions of times hotter than the center of an atomic bomb explosion. It was so super-heated that if any atoms had existed, they would have melted into electrons, protons, and neutrons, and then subsequently vaporized into upixels.

All upixels were propelled outward from the center of this explosion. But what caused the explosion? Scientists don't know whether the Big Bang was the beginning of the universe, or if it evolved from an earlier one.

A most interesting and contentious aspect of the Big Bang theory exists. In order to make the theory consistent with the vast size of the observable universe, scientists theorize that an enormous expansion of the universe occurred within an instant after the Big Bang. In the first trillionth of a trillionth of a trillionth of a second, or $10^{-36}$ seconds, the universe ballooned outward faster than the speed of light. This inflation ended ten-thousandths of a second later, $10^{-32}$ seconds after the Big Bang.

Such a brief time for expansion may not seem important. But the universe expanded by a factor of about $10^{30}$ in this instant of time. It would be like a dust particle suddenly becoming larger than the Earth. This seems like an unlikely event, and it is. Scientists still argue about whether or not, and how, such inflation could have happened.

Not only was the first fraction of a second eventful, the next few seconds led to the upixels transforming into more complex entities. As the universe expanded, so did the upixels. From the unimaginable temperatures of the Big Bang, the universe cooled sufficiently in five seconds to allow the upixels to form the nuclei of the simplest atoms, such as hydrogen. But how?

Remember, upixels are energy. I discussed how the temperature of the Big Bang would have vaporized all atoms into upixels. As the extreme temperatures cool, the process is reversed. If everything in the current universe would have been torn into upixels, the cooling of the upixels then resulted in everything in our world.

Steam when cooled becomes water which, upon further cooling, becomes ice. The process is reversible: ice when warmed becomes water and, upon additional heating, becomes steam. Scientists can explain how this happens at the molecular level—the molecules are simply behaving differently because they possess different levels of energy. What scientists have not figured out is how and why the upixels morph into more complex entities.

Some of the upixels agglomerated to become what humans later called "matter" and "particles." This occurred just five seconds after the Big Bang. These particles became protons and neutrons, the nuclei of hydrogen. Other upixels became a hot "soup," consisting of electrons and trapped light (photons). At such high energies, electrons can trap light in a plasma or soup-like substance. At this time, the nuclei of hydrogen and the soup filled the universe.

The bottom line: everything in our universe is some form of energy. The form of this energy and how these energy entities interact determine their properties, and their properties determine whether we choose to call them "matter." If we can see how existing matter can be broken down into upixels, then we can understand how upixels could have formed existing matter. In a process attempting to mimic the "hot" conditions immediately following the Big Bang, physicists are accelerating parts of atoms to nearly the speed of light and smashing them into smaller components. New, more powerful particle accelerators in the future could reveal a better understanding of the universe, including the so-called Higgs Field.

Upixels are converted into matter, but not just by cooling. In the first few moments after the Big Bang, the formation of the Higgs Field is thought to have occurred. This mysterious field engulfing the universe allows the creation of matter from the upixels. Thus, in the first few seconds after the Big Bang, the uniform upixels of the universe cooled to create the conditions for matter.

The details of creation that include formation of matter and the Higgs Field from upixels are not currently understood. The important concept is that the upixels—energy—were transformed into all these energy forms. Daunting questions remain: What is the origin of the upixels, and how were they compressed into a dot in space?

UNIVERSAL ILLUMINATION

Three hundred and eighty thousand years passed before the universe cooled sufficiently for another major change to take place.

If nuclei or atoms have too much energy or are too hot, they are unstable and cannot remain intact. Conversely, at cool enough temperatures, they can form and remain stable. When the universe cooled sufficiently, the electrons combined with the nuclei to form hydrogen, the simplest chemical element, as well as helium. As the first atoms were created, light particles were released—or, to paraphrase the Book of Genesis, light separated from darkness. Whether or not this event was a divine act, it is the longest-playing radio and TV show in the universe.

The released light broadcasts this phenomenal event by causing about one percent of the electrostatic noise we receive on a radio or television, if an antenna is used. This microwave energy or light was created 13.4 billion years ago, and it continues to inundate us from every direction.

The upixels, which came from a dot in the Big Bang, were thus transformed into hydrogen, helium, and light after 380,000 years.

## CHALLENGES TO THE BIG BANG THEORY

The Big Bang Theory is currently the most popular theory of creation, but many scientists are proposing alternate ones. Although much evidence supports the Big Bang, the theory has difficulties explaining certain concepts such as inflation. Since creation is one of the most vexing problems in science, scientists still struggle to fit the facts into a workable theory.

What are some of the new 21st-century thinking? An alternative theory to the Big Bang proposes that most of the universe did not undergo inflation. Rather, only our region of the universe—everything we can see and measure—underwent the extremely unlikely event of inflation. In this theory, think of the universe as a large tree with trillions of branches. One of the branches created a bud from a Big Bang.

Using this analogy, our universe, the bud, might be considered but one of a large number, or even an infinity, of universes. The others are beyond our awareness. In this theory, "universe" takes on a different meaning. Normally, "universe" means the total universe—all that exists. Here, "universe" instead means all we are able to perceive. To discuss the rest, scientists use the terms "multiverse" and "parallel universes." The multiverse refers to all that makes up the universe, including the parts of the universe we cannot perceive. Parallel universes refer to the other dimensions or portions of the universe beyond our detection.

Sir Roger Penrose, an Emeritus Professor of mathematics at Oxford University, who shared the Wolf Prize in physics with Stephen Hawking, calculated the odds of our particular region of the universe inflating. The odds are one in 10 to the n power ($10^n$), where n is one with 118 zeros behind it.

What does this mean? The odds calculated by Penrose can be likened to winning the mother of all lotteries. The odds of winning are not one in fifty million or even one in a billion, but one in a trillion. In this scenario, you'd have to win not once, but a hundred trillion times in a row, without losing even once. Possible, but as unlikely as you can get.

I realized then that it takes faith to believe that we live in an infinite universe, and that we won the mother of all lotteries by being in this speck of the universe that experienced the Big Bang, and the eventual creation of life. Is it really that simple?

Sir Martin Rees, Great Britain's Astronomer Royal and Royal Society Professor, speculates that too many coincidences exist in our universe. These coincidences provide evidence for the existence of perhaps millions of parallel universes. In other words, to explain these unlikely events, Sir Martin employs the concept of parallel universes, or the universe beyond our perceptive capabilities, to explain that we are just part of perhaps an infinite universe—and various parts have every property, even the property of inflation.

Though we can't be certain how the universe was created, it now seems that either the universe is infinite in size or multiple universes exist in concert with our own. Exploring these layers of reality and our relationship to them is critical if we are to understand what we are. (This discussion will occur in later chapters.)

Many other theories and variations exist, but none of them rule out a Creator or prove the existence of one. The Big Bang theory excited and delighted many who are religious by suggesting a beginning. Yet, that beginning might possess a scientific explanation, too. Even an infinite universe with no beginning or end does not rule in or rule out a Creator either. So, how can science draw any conclusions about the existence of a Creator?

CREATOR AVOIDANCE

Scientists seek to explain the birth of the universe without having to "resort" to the existence of a divine being. Perhaps Penrose summed up the opinions of many scientists when he stated:

> We might take the position that the initial choice was an 'act of God'...or we might seek some scientific/mathematical theory to explain the extraordinary special nature of the Big Bang. My own strong inclination is certainly to try to see how far we can get with the second possibility.

As I studied the seemingly strange theories, which involved numerous parallel universes and the nearly impossible odds of the creation of our world, I found that science utilizes one set of metaphors to explain the universe and religion uses another.

Understanding the creation of our world is obscured by mysteries: the Big Bang, incredibly unlikely odds of inflation, and the possibility of parallel universes. Can understanding the creation of the rest of our world shed light on our own existence?

CREATION OF STARS, CHEMICAL ELEMENTS, AND MOLECULES

The Big Bang formed hydrogen, the most prevalent element in the universe, after 380,000 years. But our world is comprised of more complex chemical elements than hydrogen. Scientists report that some of these elements, like nitrogen, were created when the first stars were formed—about 75 million years after the formation of hydrogen.

These first stars were huge, up to one 1,000 times the mass of our sun. They existed for only a few million years, unlike many of the smaller stars existing today, which live for billions of years. The nuclear fusion in these stars created immense heat and pressure resulting in the production of chemical elements. These early stars ended their lives with colossal explosions called supernovae, scattering stellar dust consisting of chemical elements like carbon, silicon, and oxygen.

The generation of additional chemical elements led to further complexity and heterogeneity in the universe. In other words, as our universe evolved, the upixels evolved into more complex entities. As new stars formed, not only were the heavier atomic elements created, but atoms also combined to form molecules such as water.

Understanding the formation of the more complex entities will help us understand our origins. Sir Arthur Eddington, an early 20th-century physicist and astronomer, noted, "For the road to a knowledge of the stars leads through the atom; and important knowledge of the atom has been reached through the stars." Indeed, all of the chemical elements in us and our world resulted from either the aftermath of the Big Bang or from nuclear reactions in stars.

THE DARK SIDE: THE CUP IS ONLY 4-PERCENT FULL

In 1998, the study of stars led to major perturbations in cosmology and physics. Scientists, by observing distant stars, found evidence that our universe is expanding faster now than before. Why? No one knows. Our universe has been increasing its rate of expansion for the last seven billion years. In an attempt to explain this, scientists have proposed the existence of dark energy.

What is dark energy? Scientists don't know. All that's known is that dark energy is responsible for pushing everything in our universe apart. Even without knowing what it is, scientists can estimate how much dark energy exists in the universe by first estimating the amount of mass therein. Then, by observing how quickly the universe is expanding, they can predict how much energy is needed to overcome gravity in order to push the universe apart at its current rate of acceleration.

This expansion requires an enormous amount of energy. If all of the matter of the universe were converted to energy used to blast the universe apart at this rate, it would not be enough. Thus, there must be vastly more dark energy than matter—more than fifteen times as much. Does this seem absurd? Michael Turner, cosmologist at the University of Chicago, says that, indeed, we live in an absurd universe. But it gets more absurd. Besides dark energy, "dark matter" lurks out there as well, and it might have been the cause of the formation of the first stars and galaxies. Dark matter is matter that projects gravitational influence on stars and galaxies, but it is "dark" by not revealing itself with the light of stars or current instruments.

In order to account for the rapid speed of stars in the outer regions of galaxies, dark matter is proposed. Otherwise, too little "normal matter" is present, and Newton's law of motion and gravity is violated. How much dark matter is needed to accommodate Sir Issac? About ten times as much as the normal matter we can measure and experience. Dark energy and dark matter are therefore not minor components of our world. Where is all this dark stuff, then? Some physicists believe the answer is: everywhere—in space, in you, and in me.

Since dark energy and dark matter are not measurable and are only inferred from their effects on our world, they are missing! Scientists believe that 96 percent of our universe is missing. It isn't as if this dark stuff was misplaced—scientists simply have not found the dark energy or dark matter that they believe exists.

Various speculations arise as to what dark matter is, but there are no leading theories. Earlier, I mentioned the Higgs Field, the energy field surrounding our universe that was created a few seconds after the Big Bang. The Higgs Field may be the source of the dark energy. This is currently a speculation, but improved particle accelerators in the next several years might provide evidence of this mysterious Higgs Field.

I was somewhat relieved to find that most scientists were as startled as I was to learn that most of our universe is "missing." In June 2003, science writer Charles Seife wrote in the journal *Science*: "It's the biggest question in physics, what is the invisible stuff blowing the universe apart?"

Many of the finest minds in physics with their arsenal of instruments have failed to find this dark stuff. The concealed dark matter and dark energy then are added to the list of the mysteries of creation. They reveal the inadequacy of current scientific theories and offer potential clues to a deeper reality.

The study of the motion of stars and galaxies has led to dark mysteries. Will understanding the origins of our solar system add even more riddles?

## OUR SOLAR SYSTEM: 9.3 BILLION YEARS AFTER THE BIG BANG

Unlike the conundrum revealed by the motion of stars and galaxies, the formation of stars such as our sun is far better understood. The creation of an environment conducive to life—like Earth—requires many unlikely events.

Our solar system is about 4.5 billion years old. The sun probably began like most stars of its size. Clouds of hydrogen gas and heavier elements such as carbon coalesced into a sphere. It is thought that sometimes a disturbance, such as the shock from a nearby supernova explosion—a massive star exploding at the end of its life—catalyzes the process, similar to the way in which the sound from a gunshot can cause an avalanche.

A young star, a few hundred thousand years old, might spin at a rate of one rotation every few days. Huge magnetic forces draw jets of dust and gas into the star. About one-tenth of the matter attracted to the star is ejected from this rotating, bulging disk. This ejection of matter gradually slows the rotation of the star—the bulge becomes the star and the disk becomes planets. Our sun has slowed to a rate of about one rotation every thirty days. The high pressures and temperatures at the center of the sun set off nuclear fusion, which is the primary energy source for life on Earth.

About a million years after the birth of our sun, disk material agglomerated into small planet-like objects called planetesimals. Violent collisions occurred between them, resulting in larger bodies, some of which became planets and moons.

An unlikely event resulted in our world having conditions for life. Some cosmologists believe that shortly after the Earth began forming, an object the size of Mars collided with it just at the correct glancing angle to send enormous quantities of debris into orbit around it. This offal coalesced into our moon. The moon is believed to be 50-60 million years younger than the Earth. Initially, it was closer to the Earth; at present, it currently has an average distance of about 235,000 miles from us.

The collision caused the axis of the Earth's rotation to be tilted out of the plane of rotation around the sun, resulting in what would become seasonal changes to our weather. The moon also stabilized the rotational axis of the Earth. This steady axis ensured that the Earth did not rotate wildly, which would have resulted in catastrophic changes in temperature and weather. Thus, the fact that we have a moon played a key role in allowing life to form and evolve on Earth.

But to understand our beginnings, we must discuss additional collisions.

The ingredients for life were present on the young Earth. Where did these ingredients come from? Some of the water on Earth came from impacts from comets and meteorites, and scientists believe that these collisions brought a host of other critical molecules essential to life. Complex molecules containing carbon were critical, since the Earth's surface possessed little carbon, and all of its life would be based on that element.

How much matter was accumulated by such collisions? About $10^{17}$ tons. This is equal to the mass of 600 million Volkswagen Beetles crashing into Earth each year for 100 million years. Even now, approximately 40,000 tons (equal to 16,000 Beetles) of interplanetary dust fall on Earth each year.

Our planet, which would harbor life, was the result of having the right-size star for a sun, our sun having planets, the Earth being the correct distance from the sun to attain optimum temperatures, and it fortuitously colliding with another planetary object, which resulted in our moon. But the early years on Earth were no bed of roses.

## LOUSY WEATHER

During the Earth's first 100-600 million years, major impacts with comets and meteorites over 100 miles in diameter resulted in hot rock vapor encompassing the globe and evaporating the oceans. Once the onslaught of collisions slowed, the planet cooled sufficiently for the water vapor from the evaporated oceans to result in a few thousand years of rain, which then created hot oceans. Due to the moon's proximity, the tides of the early Earth were enormous.

But what was the composition of the Earth's early atmosphere? Scientists are in a fog. The Earth's atmosphere contained mainly nitrogen, but scientists do not know how much methane or carbon dioxide existed. If they knew the early atmosphere's ingredients, scientists would have a better way to predict how life managed to create a foothold on early Earth.

A methane atmosphere potentially generates a million to a billion times more organic synthesis than a carbon dioxide atmosphere. Acid rain from water and high carbon dioxide content occurred for many millions of years. Whether carbon was in the form of methane or carbon dioxide, the planet now possessed the carbon necessary to create life.

We are in a universe uniquely set up for life due to the Big Bang. We live on a planet that is unique in our solar system for life as we know it, having a moon to stabilize its axis, being the optimum distance from the sun for moderate weather, and having accumulated all of the ingredients for life.

## THE SEARCH CONTINUES

Scientists have developed theories about the origin of the universe and all of its elements. However, as Neil deGrasse Tyson, an astrophysicist and director of New York City's Hayden Planetarium, states "in our attempts to uncover the history of the cosmos, we have continually discovered that the segments most deeply shrouded in mystery are those that deal with origins. "

This is true for the universe, the galaxies, and our own solar system. Scientists really do not know when or how the universe was created. And they do not know what happened to the 96 percent of our universe that is missing.

Scientific theories remain works in progress. Scientists continually modify them to take into account new discoveries. It takes faith to pursue a scientific theory—faith in the theory and scientific methodology that might reject the theory. Religion rarely engages in this practice of constant modification of concepts.

During the 20th century, the scientific theories for our creation and universe became seemingly absurd, with intimations of parallel universes, inflation, missing matter, and missing energy. Do we need these explanations? Sir John Polkinghorne, a particle physicist for more than twenty years, became a priest of the Church of England in 1979. He is also a published author on the compatibility of religion and science. Rather than arguing our good fortune to live in the one universe that happens to be conducive to life among the millions of universes, he states that our universe is "not just 'any old world,' but it's special and finely tuned for life because it is the creation of a Creator who wills that it should be so."

Five centuries ago, the knowledge that Earth was not the center of the universe sent scientists scrambling for modified theories resulting in a simpler and more convincing theory. Much of the problem of an incorrect theory of Earth's position arose from a conflict between science and religion. That conflict still remains unresolved. In the 21st century many pieces of evidence supporting the creation of our world do not fit scientific theories. This resulted in complex modifications. Can these theories evolve to simpler theories, thus healing the rift between science and spirituality?

When I began pondering our existence, I thought the exercise would be simple: find and study science's view of where we came from, what we are, and what we will become. Having done that, I would compare spiritual and religious teachings to scientific beliefs in order to arrive at the awakening I sought. Spiritualism and religion teach concepts based on faith; however, the concepts of science regarding our origins seem fantastic. I concluded that the exploration would require far deeper research.

I pondered what caused the Big Bang, and what preceded it. The great 20th-century physicist John Wheeler proposed that the universe depends upon conscious observers to make it real. This was the first of many spiritual overtones I discovered to explain our world. But who or what could have been the observer back then? I discovered that there is no "back then." In our universe, there is no interval between events in our world! (I will explain these scientific proposals later in the book.)

What caused the Big Bang? Does 4 percent of what is "out there" really create our reality? To rationalize the nearly impossible odds of the Big Bang and inflation, scientists now propose concepts of infinite and parallel universes. How do we reconcile this with our existence? We must gain a broader appreciation of reality in order to ascertain what we are and the parameters of the real universe.

Our world is made up of upixels that are a form of energy. But how does all this lead to life?

The origin of life is part of the mystery of our origins. I believed that an understanding of life's origins would yield clues to reality. What I did not and could not anticipate were the surprises awaiting me.

*The cosmos is all that is or ever was or ever will be... We know that we are approaching the greatest of mysteries.*

—Carl Sagan

# 2
# LIFE

*I'm absolutely convinced that no one should die of leukemia.*
*And I refuse to concede a patient's life without doing something*
*if the patient wants to be saved.*

–Robert Peter Gale

What is "life?" One definition is an organism that can grow, re-produce, and have a metabolism (ongoing chemical reactions) as opposed to a dead organism, or inanimate matter. While this may seem fairly straightforward, it excludes some elements that we may instinctively consider alive. Are seeds that lie dormant for years alive? If they are not, what defines the instant in which they become "alive?" If seeds are already alive, what makes them so? No chemical reactions are occurring, i.e. no signs of life.

And what about so-called gram-positive bacteria that run out of nutrients? When they sense that they cannot continue to live, they put their biochemical energy into creating spores. In harsh environments, gram-positive bacteria cease to exist after creating spores. Are bacterial spores alive? Spores, like seeds, can remain dormant for decades with no signs of chemical reactions. Then, they spring to life as bacteria when the environment supplies nutrients, proper environmental conditions, and moisture. These bacteria are genetically identical to the bacteria that produced spores. If spores are not alive, then what confers life to them resulting in live bacteria?

All of these questions about life lead to the ultimate question, what is death? What is the difference between the instant before death and the instant after? Valuable information about life comes from studies of death and disease. Because of my personal experiences, I connect death with cancer and disease.

Life in animals results from the correct amount of cell growth and division, followed by moderation or cessation of cell proliferation. We grow from a single cell to fetus to child to adult and stop growing. Pathogens infect all forms of life and lead to death. It is critical for bacteria and all forms of life to have defenses against infective entities. In humans, one of the numerous defenses to infection and disease are white blood cells, which are produced from bone marrow. These cells manufacture antibodies to fight disease, and even engulf and devour bacteria, preventing infection.

In the case of leukemia, white blood cells become abnormal and are overproduced. Huge numbers of abnormal white blood cells hijack the body's resources, leading to death. Leukemia and all cancers result from abnormal cells and uncontrolled cell proliferation. The typical cancer treatment in the 1980s used some sort of poison to kill cells. Even radiation used in bone marrow transplantation and for other cancer treatments is lethal to cells. Because the cancer cells grow faster than normal cells, the goal was to kill off the cancer before killing the patient. Due to their potentially poisonous nature, candidate drugs needed to be tested for safety as a first step in clinical trials.

Only terminally ill cancer patients are allowed to participate in many cancer clinical trials, and must sign documents stating they accept the risks.

Cancer patients often suffer from pain and experience a variety of health problems brought on by their weakened bodies. The anguish of patients I met depressed me. The vast majority is middle-aged or elderly, but some types of cancer, such as several types of leukemia, strike the young. Leukemia was the primary focus of 10 West.

I returned after a year to visit Bob Gale. I knew many of the patients I previously encountered at his ward might have relapsed or died.

Still, I wanted to believe that Doris had survived and was doing well. I recalled her penetrating eyes, animated gestures, and passion—and her emotional plea for a cure. I knew her appearance would have changed with the treatment, but I refused to imagine Doris looking any different from when I last saw her.

In my time visiting cancer wards, whenever I became depressed, I would cheer myself up by thinking of Doris's smile and zest. Upon returning to 10 West, I was anxious to learn her fate. She had died a month earlier. The details did not register—just the fact that she had died. I left 10 West shortly after.

Bob Gale probably did not detect any visible change in me that day. We had become friends, and he advised me in matters regarding medicine and cancer. Together with a leading biotechnology firm, my company developed anticancer drugs, and I had visited numerous cancer centers to witness the clinical-trial stages of new drugs. There are over a hundred different diseases that are categorized as cancer. Despite headlines in the press about the promise of the new wonder drugs from biotechnology, it was highly unlikely that one particular regime would be the magic bullet to cure all.

That night, after visiting 10 West, I wandered around the Holiday Inn, where I was staying. I felt lost. I should have been happy with my career and life. I had always dreamed of becoming a scientist, and now I was heading research and development for a company in one of the most exciting fields in science—medical biotechnology.

I thought about what I was trying to accomplish with my career and what I wanted to do in life. I don't know how long I walked or where I went that evening. Back in my room, I decided that I wanted to understand the definition of life and what happened after death. I needed to know what had happened to Doris. And, for the first time in decades, I thought about Stanley's funeral.

I gazed at the sky that night, attempting to recover from the shock of Doris's fate. I wondered what was really out there. After death, are the only remnants of the deceased ashes and a few memories held by the living? Is there meaning and a plan for us as the religious and spiritual teach?

I felt that I had to better understand what life was before I could tackle the mystery of death. How did star "stuff" become life? If there are trillions of universes, are only a few capable of life? Are the missing dark matter and dark energy involved in life?

Could a better understanding of life's origins help me understand Stanley's and Doris's fate—or anyone else's?

## WHERE DID WE COME FROM?

Though scientists do not know what the upixels of the universe are, where they came from, or how they became more complex entities, upixels transformed into atoms and molecules. Somehow, early Earth had all the correct chemicals. So how did these chemicals assemble to form life?

A simple single-cell bacterium carries hundreds of complex proteins and several million bits of information in its genetic makeup that encodes its life processes. The possibility of creating just one protein that makes up life is extremely remote.

In their simulations of the early Earth, no scientist has succeeded in converting simple chemical ingredients into just one of these complex molecules. Sir Fred Hoyle, a renowned astrophysicist and mathematician of the 20th century, likened the probability of random emergence of single-celled life to the probability of a Boeing 747 assembling as the result of a tornado whirling through a junkyard.

As with the creation of the universe, the creation of life is a focal point for science and religion, not merely a source of conflict. Unlike the creation of the universe, which many believe is explained by one widely accepted scientific theory, there is no dominant scientific theory of life's creation in existence. None of the proposals can even be called a theory since insufficient evidence exists to support any of them. And none of these speculations provide evidence for or against a creator.

The word "faith" is normally reserved for spirituality and religion. However, scientific speculations about the creation of life also require a kind of faith, since no evidence or even a solid theory describes how life originated. In this instance, both science and religion rely on faith.

## A DEFINITION OF LIFE

What defines life? What happens when a bag of chemicals, a bacterial spore, begins to produce chemical reactions and "lights up" a life? This process also becomes important when we consider death and the possibility of an afterlife. What, exactly, is extinguished when we die?

Of life and its definition, what do the scientific experts think? Francis Crick, Nobel Prize winner and a co-discoverer of the double-helix structure of DNA, defined life as having:

1) The ability to replicate both its own instructions and any machinery needed to execute the self-replication.
2) Relatively error-free replication of genetic information.
3) Close proximity of genes and their protein products?
4) A supply of energy.

Life, therefore, is defined as something that is self-replicating, even though it might be quite different from the organisms that exist on Earth. Life must have proteins or some other chemicals capable of catalyzing important chemical reactions. It must also have some form of genetic information.

A catalyst is a substance that accelerates a chemical reaction without being affected itself. Many of the chemical reactions needed for life require catalysts because of the mild conditions present in the organism. Without catalysts, many chemical reactions that sustain living organisms would require scorching temperatures and extreme pressures. With life's catalysts, these reactions occur at room temperature or colder and at normal atmospheric conditions.

Imagine driving a car over a mountain range. A tunnel has been constructed so that you do not need to ascend over 3,000 feet of mountain terrain. The tunnel is like a catalyst in that the energy to propel your car up 3,000 feet is not required to get to the other side. Many of life's catalysts are unique proteins. However, non-protein catalysts could have been responsible for first life.

The requirements for life, according to Crick, do not address the particular molecules required for life.

What complex molecules are essential for life? This seems like a straightforward question, especially when we consider the advances in biochemistry and molecular biology. We know quite well the essential molecules that are necessary for the functions and replication of current living organisms. But since the young Earth had no oxygen and the environment was extremely hostile by modern standards, we cannot identify the first life forms. This makes it impossible to know what chemicals they utilized.

This brings me to the leading speculations of science regarding the origins of life. To understand first life, scientists are examining how first life might have resulted from chemical ingredients. All of the leading scientific hypotheses involve chemicals found on Earth, chemicals provided from space, or organisms produced in space.

Let's create life. We have an imaginary cell, a membrane bag in which to assemble a bunch of chemicals. What do we need? According to Crick, we need chemical instructions such as proteins, RNA or DNA (both RNA and DNA are nucleic acids and found in current living organisms), and chemicals that can replicate or copy the instructions and supply energy. Numerous sources of energy existed on the young planet: there was sunlight, as well as a variety of chemicals that could have reacted in the bag to yield energy. The challenge is to determine the source of information and what catalysts were available that copied the instructions and allowed the energy-producing reactions to occur.

Could first life have been the result of random chemical synthesis of proteins? Proteins are even more complex than RNA or DNA,
as there are twenty different amino acids that make up the building
blocks of proteins. Out of the nearly infinite number of combinations
possible, only a minuscule fraction is useful for living organisms.

Although amino acids, the building blocks of proteins, can be created in the laboratory—and are found in meteorites and comets—it is
not clear how they could have been combined into the proteins essential for life. As Hoyle said, the chances are extremely small. Even if it
did happen one time, it would lead to only one protein. Hundreds are
needed for life. Yet life appeared on Earth a relatively short time after
the planet's formation.

So, if proteins were not the key factors in the origin of life, what
are the other possibilities?

Some scientists believe an earlier, simpler form of RNA was present to cause life. Harvard professor Andrew Knoll suggested that a
simple RNA molecule might be made from amino acids and simplified nucleic acids. We would need some evidence, however, that it
could easily be generated in the conditions on early Earth and that
such molecules can self-replicate.

Recently, one of the simpler forms of RNA was shown to self-as-
semble into a longer molecule, but it was still far too small to be an
RNA information source. However, the recent progress represents a
step toward explaining how RNA-like compounds might have been
produced and could have been the basis for life.

Leslie Orgel, a scientist at the Salk Institute, is optimistic that "the
gap will begin to close as chemists and molecular biologists pursue
their collaborative research programs." Significant clues to life's beginnings are expected from the studies of objects from space, including
meteors and comets.

For it may be that the chemicals necessary for life did not form
on Earth but came from space. What contributions did such objects
make to first life's bag of chemicals?

Meteorites and comets contributed to Earth's early oceans and could have provided considerable complex organic compounds. Such compounds, including amino acids, can take one of two forms. The type found in meteorites is called "L," which is the form found in living systems. More than seventy amino acids, as well as numerous complex organic compounds, were found on the Murchison meteorite, which struck Earth in 1969. Several of the amino acids had a predominance of the L form. Numerous other amino acids not normally found in life on Earth were found in this meteorite.

Through this work, which started in 1970 and was carried out over the next two decades, the extraterrestrial source of the molecules was verified by evidence from multiple areas of research and by numerous researchers. Biochemist John Cronin at Arizona State University believes that the Murchison meteorite adds "a new dimension" to our understanding of where critical molecules came from.

UNIVERSAL CHEMISTRY

Could simple compounds yield complex molecules in space, and thus provide clues to how life began? Could the dark endless sky we see above be the giant Petri dish in which it all started?

Several decades ago, I co-invented a method of producing molecules in the laboratory, using a simple inorganic salt as a catalyst to convert methanol into complex organic compounds. This work and the laboratory results from numerous other researchers provide evidence that simple compounds such as carbon monoxide, carbon dioxide, and methanol can react to yield larger molecules in space.

Indeed, scientists have discovered many elaborate hydrocarbons in meteorites. These are the kinds of compounds that provide building blocks for more complex molecules necessary for life and, in all likelihood, many of these compounds, such as amino acids, were provided by collisions. Scientists are beginning to look for clues in space objects such as comets.

These explorations should reveal the sorts of complex molecules delivered from space. Thus, scientists need a better understanding of the composition of meteors and comets. What better way than to go out there and take a sample? Beginning in 2005, space probes brought back samples to Earth. Scientists are currently sifting through data for clues to the organic debris that landed on the young Earth.

### MICROMETEORITES: SMALL OBJECTS, MAJOR CLUES?

So-called micrometeorites were a source of early material on Earth. When the solar system formed, these small meteorites (less than five meters in size) were prevalent in space.

The micrometeorites carried their own "heat shields," which became partially consumed upon entering the Earth's atmosphere. They gradually decelerated, and dust-sized particles floated down from the atmosphere. Protected by the shield, these micrometeorites contained amino acids and many complex organic compounds.

As much as 500 tons a year of organic compounds may have been delivered by micrometeorites during Earth's first several million years. Hunters of micrometeorites have traveled from Greenland to Antarctica to study this unique class of extraterrestrial material.

Incredibly, the micrometeorites contained metals and possessed catalytic properties. Their unique physical structure could have catalyzed many chemical reactions on early Earth. As the new chemical reactions occurred, new chemical resources were created for life on our planet.

The micrometeorite particles were quite porous and acted as molecular sponges. These "sponges" could have absorbed complex organic molecules once on Earth. Michel Maurette, an astrophysicist from Orsay, France, and an expert on micrometeorites, believes the roles that these particles played involved delivering key ingredients for life, absorbing organic compounds, catalyzing reactions, and yielding complex precursors to living organisms.

ARE THE SEEDS OF OUR EXISTENCE STILL WITH US?

Obviously, life somehow existed on a young Earth. Is it possible that early primitive forms of life still exist? Could they now be lurking somewhere, evolving even newer life forms? Could we find these early forms if they still exist on Earth?

The early Earth had no oxygen in its atmosphere. The first microbes may have long ago died out, mutated, or migrated to rare locations with no oxygen, perhaps underground or deep in the oceans. In fact, the deep subterranean bacterial biomass is estimated to equal the total bacterial biomass on the surface of Earth. If the relics still exist, how could we detect them? If found, they would yield valuable information as to how life began.

Researchers would first have to locate these relics. Then they would have to do extensive searching into environments that would have been protected from oxygen for several billion years, such as deep in the Earth. Scientists would also need to collect the samples without exposing them to any oxygen. They would need to know what chemicals and environment to provide in order to allow them to thrive. So far, no one has found organisms with unusual RNA or other unusual chemical compounds suggesting that they represent first life.

Up to this point, I have discussed how life might have emerged on Earth from chemicals. But did it? An alternate explanation is that life came from space. Since scientists have not found organisms with unusual or simple forms of proteins, RNA, or DNA, I conclude that first life died out, is in hiding, or already had the complex molecules found in organisms today. If the first creatures possessed the complicated molecules of today, many scientists would suggest they came from space. Exobiology is a recent science which attempts to find evidence for living organisms in space.

## DID LIFE COME FROM SPACE?

The question of whether life originated on Earth, or was seeded from space, is an important one. Our sun is about 4.5 billion years old. Since the observable universe is about fourteen billion years old, other solar systems may have developed life well before our sun existed.

The investigation of space objects might reveal how life started on Earth. Of all the other planets and over 140 moons in our solar system, so far, only one planet, Mars, and two moons, Titan and Europa, have properties which interest scientists who are questioning how life began on Earth. Titan, a moon of the planet Saturn, is the only other sizable object in our solar system found to have an atmosphere of significant gases—one possibly like that found on our early planet. As on Earth, the most common component in Titan's atmosphere is nitrogen.

The organic compounds found on Titan, Europa, and other extraterrestrial objects should provide a better idea of the organic compounds on early Earth. That information could lead to clues about how life formed here.

## LIFE ON THE RED PLANET?

At the time Earth was being bombarded with meteorites and comets, Mars was also being pummeled. Many of these objects brought water. Present as streams and oceans, it was believed to have been present on Mars during its early years. While the surface of Mars is now a desert, much of that water should still be in the polar icecaps and under the surface. Liquid water might house microorganisms similar to those on early Earth.

Throughout Mars's history, impacts with other objects have caused material on its surface to be ejected into space. Some of that material is drawn by gravity to Earth. These meteorites may show us that life was also generated on Mars. Some scientists even speculate that Martian life was the source of life on Earth.

In fact, 35 meteorites on Earth are believed to have come from Mars. David McKay of NASA has suggested that one of these meteorites has evidence of past life on the red planet. The subject is much debated, but future missions to Mars may resolve the issue. In the next few decades several missions are planned by NASA and the European Space Agency. Many scientists believe our best chance of finding evidence of life beyond Earth is through further exploration of Mars. Is it possible that the primitive organisms that may still exist somewhere on Earth might be easier found by spending billions of dollars to explore planets and their moons?

### PLACE YOUR BETS: THE ODDS OF LIFE

The hypothesis that life first formed elsewhere in our vast universe was suggested by Sir Fred Hoyle and Chandra Wickramasinghe, astrophysicists and mathematicians, in 1979. Later, they felt that the odds were too low for this to have happened, based on the unlikely probability of creating protein enzymes. Their estimation was $10^{-40,000}$.

One can quibble about a few zeroes, but one divided by one followed by 40,000 zeroes is a very low chance. But, let's put this into perspective. It would be similar to the lottery mentioned in Chapter 1, where the odds of winning were one in a trillion. In this case, however, you would have to win "only" about a thousand times in a row, not the 100 trillion times in a row required for the universe's inflation, according to Penrose.

If scientists generally subscribe to the idea that we won the mother of all lotteries, which led to inflation, why shouldn't they accept the possibility of life from the far less improbable manner suggested by Hoyle and Wickramasinghe? In other words, although these odds might be too low for spontaneous generation of the correct proteins on Earth, the odds are better if one considers the vast numbers of objects in the universe for many billions of years before Earth existed. Furthermore, life could have begun in several ways other than from protein progenitor molecules.

Neil deGrasse Tyson, an astrophysicist and director of New York City's Hayden Planetarium, offers a rather simple set of criteria for life:

1. It has a source of energy.

2. It must contain sufficient atoms to be able to create complex structures (molecules).

3. There must exist some liquid solvent for the molecules to interact in, like water or some other liquid.

4. There must be sufficient time for life to arise.

Given these requirements, it seems that a huge number of opportunities existed before our solar system was formed.

## WHAT WAS FIRST LIFE ON EARTH, AND HOW DID IT OCCUR?

My reaction to the lack of a theory on the origin of life was a disappointment. Then I realized that, unlike many other areas of science, such as astronomy and biology, this field is quite young. J. William Schoff, professor of paleobiology at UCLA, points out:

> With active research dating only from the 1950s the field is
> young, vibrant and advancing rapidly. Given time, effort, and
> a continuing influx of imaginative students and fresh ideas,
> we can one day fully answer the *what*, *when*, and *how* of life's
> beginnings.

The creation of the universe is all about mathematical odds. The odds of creating the correct molecules to produce life are extremely low. However, the extremely low odds of the Big Bang and inflation are overcome with the rationale of an infinite universe and parallel universes.

Therefore, solving the riddle of the origin of life might involve looking into the theories of the origin of the universe. The payoff could be reconciling science and spirituality. The unlikely odds of life's creation can be overcome with enough chances. With billions of potential sources of life for nine billion years, the odds become better.

First life might have originated in some of the billions of stars hosting planets before our sun existed. The materials for our solar system came from debris from expired stars and possibly their planets. Life might have hitchhiked with the debris. But this is speculation.

## WHAT ABOUT A CREATOR?

As one examines the various suggestions for the origin of life, it is obvious that no one explanation contains sufficient evidence to be called a theory. Certainly, a Nobel Prize awaits the first breakthrough. And none of these hypotheses exclude the possibility of a Creator.

The scientists attempting to explain the creation of life through natural processes have faith that, indeed, such processes existed. Iris Fry, author of *The Emergence of Life on Earth* and a teacher at the Cohn Institute at Tel Aviv University, wrote:

> As long as no scientific theory has succeeded in providing a fully convincing account of the emergence of life on Earth, the adoption of an evolutionary point of view toward the question of life's origin and the rejection of the idea of purposeful design involves a very strong philosophical commitment.

Stated simply, just as it takes faith to believe in a Creator, it also takes faith to believe in life's beginning without a Creator.

The issue of whether or not a Creator existed does not have to cause a rift between science and spirituality. Scientists do not have evidence to reject the concept of a Creator, and spiritualists need not feel threatened by the beliefs of science. The spiritual awakening that Matthew Fox stated at the beginning of Chapter 1 might be achievable if the rift between science and spirituality could be healed.

In thinking of a Creator, many look to a God-like entity placing life on Earth. If we accept the metaphoric nature of science and
religious teachings, then perhaps a Creator, in His infinite wisdom,
created a multitude of universes, knowing that life would spring up in
one or more of them.

## UPIXELS, BAGS, ENERGY, AND LIFE

In conclusion, the upixels of the universe began to transform into more
complex entities just a few seconds after the Big Bang. They formed
simple atoms. These collected into stars. The stars created the rest of
the chemical elements. Those elements combined to form molecules.
Transformations of ever-increasing complexity represent an evolution
of the upixels into all we experience in the universe, including ourselves.

Scientists do not know how the upixels, a form of energy, resulted
in life. Did the mere rolling of the dice on a billion, billion places in
the universe for billions of years result in life from energy? Or is there
some pre-programmed feature of the upixels that tip the odds in favor
of life? Whatever the case, energy somehow led to life. All life requires
linked networks of complex chemical reactions that transform energy.
In other words, life involves transforming energy in a defined, confined space.

If, as scientists, we don't know what first life was, perhaps we can
understand how it began. It turns out that all bacteria currently on
Earth pump protons across their membrane "bag" to create energy akin
to a miniature battery, in the same way pumping water up a mountain
into a dam creates an energy potential since the dammed water can
then produce hydroelectric energy. The reservoir of protons creates an
electrical potential, and all bacteria produce such electrochemical energy. Microbes use numerous sources of energy such as the sun, inorganic chemicals, and organic chemicals to pump the protons.

Since it is widely assumed that present-day bacteria are the descendants of original life, it can be assumed that early life utilized available energy sources to pump upixels across membranes. But how were the first bags of chemicals bestowed with life? I reflected on the consciousness proposed by Wheeler, which converts upixels and the Big Bang into reality. If this is true, did consciousness help create first life? How could consciousness precede life? Then I recalled that scientists believe that time is a myth and all times exist out there. Since this is such an important concept, I will discuss it in more detail in Chapter 5.

To date, an examination of our origins has not given insight as to where we came from. Instead, we are confounded with more mysteries.

As for the difference between life and death, we will continue the discussion in later chapters on reality and the afterlife.

What happens if we move beyond the issue of first life? Unlike the relatively new science of life's beginnings, evolution has been studied by scientists for over a century. Evolution, another battleground between science and many religious theorists, is central to the question of where we came from. Is evolution fraught with uncertainty and mystery like the creation of the universe and the origin of life? Actually, it can provide a fascinating clue to understanding life.

> *The first peace, which is the most important, is that which comes within the souls of people when they realize their relationship, their oneness, with the universe and all its powers, and when they realize at the center of the universe dwells the Great Spirit, and that this center is really everywhere, it is within each of us.*

> —Black Elk

# 3
# EVOLUTION

*I do not think it possible to get anywhere if we start from skepticism. We must start from a broad acceptance of whatever seems to be knowledge and is not rejected for some specific reason.*

—Bertrand Russell

Evolution has produced a bewildering diversity of life, which exists in some of the strangest and most unimaginable places. Some creatures live in hydrothermal vents at the bottom of the ocean. Temperatures there exceed 300 degrees Fahrenheit, and the pressure is thousands of times greater than our surface environment—and lethal to all animals on the surface of the Earth. So-called ice worms can live in the arctic ice at temperatures below freezing. They melt and die when "warmed" to a few degrees above freezing.

Evolution thrives on opportunity. This is illustrated by organisms evolving and surviving in extreme environments in oceans, in ice, below ground, and on Earth's surface. This auspicious feature of life and evolution results in organisms being predatory, parasitic, or synergistic.

Many people believe that the ongoing evolution of other species is not relevant to human existence. This is not the case. At least a hundred trillion microbes live on and in adult humans. This is more than the number of human cells. Bacteria are less than a thousandth the size of a human cell, viruses even smaller. We need many of the bacteria living in us to survive. Trillions of bacteria in the gut are needed to digest our food and trillions of other bacteria colonize various parts of our oral cavities and produce antibiotic agents, which suppress pathogens.

Many people are surprised that, in co-evolving with these microbes, we have emerged as nature's most complex composite organism. Humans are a mosaic of human cells, beneficial bacteria, other microbes living in and on us, and pathogens. Bacterial infections cause ulcers and heart disease, while viral infections are implicated in several forms of cancer. Pathogenic bacteria, viruses, and other microbes that invade humans are opportunistic and contain the potential to wipe out our existence. Fortunately, evolution has also provided us with a complex array of defenses called the immune system, which allows our bodies to recognize and destroy disease-causing agents through the implementation of specialized cells and immunochemicals.

These defenses are the result of evolution, in which the body's most effective chemical agents combat the latest invaders that evolution has also produced. The ongoing battle between evolving immune-defense molecules and newly evolved pathogens is the quintessential example of the ultimate evolutionary struggle for survival of the fittest.

My job was to find and utilize natural human defenses to combat diseases like cancer. Unlike typical poisons used in cancer treatment, these immunochemicals are non-lethal to humans. The biotechnology revolution allows the isolation and production of these defense molecules. Biotechnology relies on the theory of evolution to help find these molecules, like a beacon showing the way.

Many important genes and biochemicals were first discovered in animals or other organisms. A race then ensued to find the human counterpart. In evolution, when comparing the genes from different organisms, the more similar the genes, the closer the life forms are on the evolutionary tree. In providing defenses for cancer and illness, animals developed immune responses. Interferon, one type of molecule to fight illness, is found in mice and many other animals, including humans. The interferon molecules vary slightly among different species.

Monkey interferon, for instance, is more similar to that of humans than mouse interferon.

As a research and development director, I was in charge of developing new drugs as well as coming up with the strategy for future efforts. My company was in a race with others to genetically engineer human interferon, a family of natural defense molecules for treatment of diseases such as cancer and multiple sclerosis. I had toured the few existing biotechnology companies with the president of research, and we convinced the executives at my company to make a fifty-million-dollar commitment to one of them.

This particular company had engineered bacteria to produce interferon. We then invested additional funds to build a huge fermentation facility to make enough interferon for clinical trials. Human interferon is produced in healthy individuals to fight disease, even cancer. We hoped that by producing the compounds in bacteria and giving them in high doses to humans, diseases such as cancer and multiple sclerosis could be controlled without the side effects of most chemical drugs.

It turned out that several different kinds of human interferon existed. In order to better understand this exciting technology, I worked in the laboratory and helped isolate a few of the interferon genes. A decade passed before one would be marketed for the treatment of multiple sclerosis. Interferon reduces relapses, and has shown improved quality of life and cognitive function in MS patients.

After my work with interferon, I was involved both as a scientist and VP of research in the studies of the evolution of a bacterium. The diversity we found in this simple organism was enormous and became the subject of many publications and patents. The biotechnology revolution, which utilized molecular biology to understand and treat human diseases, also led to understanding differences between various life forms at the genetic level. Understanding evolution can lead to a better understanding of our existence, since the evolutionary path to humans was a complex process involving interdependent co-evolution.

## WHY THIS BATTLEGROUND?

Beyond the conflict between science and religion concerning the creation of the universe and origin of life, another contentious topic concerns how humans came to be. Unlike the creation of the universe or first life, evolution is accepted by scientists and is generally not considered controversial within their ranks. On the other hand, in nearly every topic we will cover, there are mysteries, enigmas, and inconsistencies. Still, the riddles and paradoxes of evolution are minor compared to those found in other areas of science. And evolution can help us understand life and how we were created.

## A TIME PERSPECTIVE OF EVOLUTION

Scientists generally admit that they do not know what form first life took, how it began, or if a Creator was involved. But scientists have discovered the approximate times various living organisms appeared on Earth, and have found significant evidence to support evolution theory.

Shown below on Table 1: the approximate time (in millions of years ago) the life form appeared, what particular event occurred, and comments on the significance of the event.

Table 1. Evolution of life on Earth

| Age (Mil./yrs ago) | Event | Comments |
|---|---|---|
| ? | First life | Unknown as to whether DNA or RNA was present in this organism, origin unknown. |
| 1,900-3,900 | Cyanobac-teria-like organisms | Used carbon dioxide to create oxygen which eventually led to our oxygen atmosphere. |

| 720 | Clams | Early brain. |
|---|---|---|
| 544-543 | Explosion of new life forms. | Eyes. |
| 251 | Mass extinc-tion of spe-cies | 80-95% of species became extinct. |
| 220 | Bees | Beginning of social insects. |

EVOLUTION OF LIFE ON EARTH: WHEN DID IT START?

Some scientists believe life first began as early as 3.9 billion years ago, as some fossils indicate. Because this is only 500 million years after Earth formed, scientists puzzle over how life could have formed so quickly. If life was seeded from space, this timing might be logical, but some individuals have used this "quick start of life" as evidence of a Creator, arguing that sufficient time for natural processes to lead to life would not have existed.

However, the only evidence that is generally accepted is fossil evidence from about 1.9 billion years ago, which is roughly 2.5 billion years after Earth formed. The case for an earlier date of first life is becoming stronger with new evidence of fossils of 3.5 billion years ago from various sources.

The Theory of Evolution holds that an organism adapts to the environment, and, through mutations, develops offspring that become more adaptable. However, among early life, genes were somehow freely exchanged and, therefore, what evolved was a community of diverse organisms swapping genes. This is still true today since bacteria rapidly exchange genes.

Why is this information important? Because it reveals the degree to which all life is related and interdependent.

## EARTH'S EARLY LIFE

Early Earth was literally a different world, having no oxygen, hot oceans, suffocating atmospheric pressures, and constant bombardment by comets and meteorites. Whether first life came from space or emerged from ingredients on Earth, here is what we do know:

1. Between 3.9 billion years ago and 1.9 billion years ago, cyanobacteria appeared and transformed our planet. They converted light, water, and carbon dioxide into oxygen and organic material. Oxygen in our atmosphere did not reach its current levels until around 600 million years ago.

2. Whatever defined first life, it evolved to yield microbes that became highly adaptable. First life and early organisms were "bags" of chemicals, which performed simple life functions, such as reproduction.

All early life is believed to have been microbes composed of single cells—living "bags" of chemicals capable of generating electrochemical energy. Today, bacteria can be found within larger bacteria. This is a clue to what happened about 1.5 billion years ago—single cells evolved into organisms that contained a bag within the bag. This new bag, a nucleus, was a membrane around the microbe's DNA.

Other membrane-like structures also appeared. These different kinds of bags within the cell allowed functions to be separated. The nucleus housed the reproductive machinery, mitochondria contained energy-producing components, and chloroplasts harbored specialized chemicals that converted sunlight, carbon dioxide, and water into sugars and oxygen. As a consequence of these bags within cells, life was poised to become even more complex.

The mitochondria and chloroplasts originated from captured microbes. The original bacterium that became mitochondria even donated most of its genes to the host's nucleus as modern DNA analysis indicates. The evolution of bacteria thus led to conglomerate organisms. With such internal bags, organisms could become thousands of times larger than bacteria due to hundreds or thousands of mitochondria producing energy via proton pumps.

The one-celled organisms with their specialized "bags" subsequently clustered into colonies. Modern amoebas still have this feature—the ability to cluster into slime mold. Just as with compartmentalization of functions within cells, bags led to more complex organisms and clusters of cells led to more elaborate creatures. I call these clusters "sacks."

The first sack developed around a billion years ago. It was a stalk-like structure encasing groups of cells. This evolved to other multi-celled, more complex organisms whose cells were many thousand times larger than bacteria. These had several different sacks of specialized cells, with each one performing specialized functions. The result: organs and various body parts. Simple body plans appeared with a mouth, a gut, and a gelatinous body. One example is the clam, which came into existence 720 million years ago. Clams even possess an early form of a brain.

The evolution of animals progressed slowly up to 544 million year ago. At that time, Earth had only three divisions (or types) of animals, called phyla. At this slow rate, it would have been difficult to explain the evolution to complex organisms such as humans.

## EARTH'S "EXPLOSION" OF NEW ORGANISMS

However, between 544 and 543 million years ago, the number of phyla jumped from three to 38. Archeologists made this discovery when fossils uncovered in Canada and in other parts of the world indicated an "explosion" of new animals. This explosion baffled Charles Darwin, who realized that it embodied potential evidence counter to his theory of evolution. During the 19th and 20th centuries, this mystery continued to confound scientists, and no satisfying theory emerged. Then, at the dawn of the 21st century, a theory was proposed that seems to be quite plausible.

Andrew Parker, a researcher at the University of Oxford, in his 2003 book *In the Blink of an Eye*, theorized that the explosion in life forms resulted from organisms obtaining eyes, the most recent sack of specialized cells. Rather than relying solely on feel and chemical receptors to sense their environments, animals possessed vision, however limited. Sight enabled the easier capture of prey and early warning against predators. Eyes also allowed organisms to visually learn from and mimic each other. This development, which occurred 543 million years ago, of our most-used sense, sight, helped to form us. Up to that point, life had known five key events:

1. The beginning of life on Earth (still a mystery);

2. The formation of the nucleus and other organelles;

3. The rise of multi-cellular organisms;

4. The specialization of organs such as brains;

5. The appearance of eyes.

Parker's theory seemed to answer all the questions except one: What triggered the evolution of the eye? We don't know. Often, science solves one puzzle only to discover another.

In disputing evolution, some religious groups have demanded "missing links," life forms halfway between two known species that would prove one evolved into the other. For example, they wanted evidence that sea creatures adapted to land. In 2006 such a link was found; scientists discovered fishlike fossils bearing limbs that lived about 385 million years ago.

According to fossil records dating back 251 million years, the most dramatic mass extinction on record occurred: perhaps as many as 95 percent of all species, both on land and sea, perished. Dinosaurs became extinct about 65 million years ago, perhaps from an asteroid collision with Earth, which resulted in climate changes and the destruction of plant life.

Some religious groups accept that animals do evolve, but they do not accept the concept of man evolving from the ape. Let's examine what is known.

FROM APE TO HUMAN

The evolution of humans from apelike ancestors is believed to have started about five to six million years ago. These creatures had brains about a third the size of humans'. About 2.5 to 1.8 million years ago, *Homo erectus* came on the scene. *Erectus* had a larger brain, though only about half the size of a modern human's. He used tools and had a simple language. This erectus is believed to have moved from Africa to Europe about 800,000 years ago. One hundred fifty thousand years ago, *Homo neanderthalensis* appeared, having a brain about the same size as ours. Then, about 100,000-150,000 years ago, probably in Africa, humans, known as *Homo sapiens*, emerged.

Around 70,000 years ago, the climate changed due to a super volcanic eruption in an area that is now Indonesia. This event nearly wiped out *Homo sapiens*, reducing their numbers to only a few thousand on the African continent. About 40,000-60,000 years ago, they moved out of Africa, and 40,000 years ago, started using language and many new tools. About 10,000-15,000 years ago, humans moved into the Americas via the frozen bridge between Siberia and Alaska. Recent evidence shows that *erectus* and *neanderthalensis* became extinct at different times on different continents.

Table 2. An abbreviated summary of the evolution of humans

| Age | Ape ancestor | Comments |
|---|---|---|
| 5-6 million years ago | Common ancestor of current African apes and man | This ancestor has not been identified as yet |
| 4 to 2.5 million years ago | *A. afarensis* | Known as Lucy |

| 2 million years ago | *H. habilis, H. rudolfensis & H. ergaster* | Has larger brain than earlier apes |
|---|---|---|
| 1.8 million years ago | *H. erectus* | Brain volume is about double that of earlier apes |
| 150,000 years ago | *H. neanderthalensis* | Larger brain than *H. erectus* |
| 100,000 years ago | *H. sapiens sapiens* | Modern humans |

Animals with eyes learned by mimicking each other. Memes, ideas learned from others, could be behavior or a tune for animals, or a phrase for humans. Although verbal memes were probably also utilized by more primitive species, human use of language created language memes, which allowed a more rapid transmission of complex information. Of all the "sacks" of cells, the larger brain of humans allowed for talking, learning, understanding language, and organizing complex information.

Language is believed to have played a significant role in human evolution. Language and memes probably led to the use of tools. About 10,000 years ago, humans began using tools in agriculture. They also domesticated animals and plants.

Scientists search for explanations to evolution in the way of specific mechanisms. How did all of the evolutionary changes occur?

## THE MECHANISM FOR EVOLUTION: DNA SHUFFLING, REARRANGEMENT, AND MUTATIONS

Organisms adapted to the changing environment and found increasingly sophisticated solutions to the problems posed by life. But how did these adaptations occur?

We can see the mechanism in action in a common soil bacteri-um—a gram-positive bacterium that develop spores, which I men-tioned at the beginning of Chapter 2. However, the species that drew my attention and interest also evolved to produce an insecticide.

My research group and others found thousands of different strains of this common bacterium on every continent. At the time when it ran out of nutrients and should have put all of its biochemical resources into creating spores, this bacterium devoted half of its energy to mak-ing insecticidal proteins. But why? If the survival of the species de-pended on the bacterium producing a viable spore before it died, why divert valuable resources to produce an insecticidal protein?

Specific genes produced these proteins. We found over a hundred variations in these genes produced through mutations. These different genes allowed each strain to produce a unique insecticidal protein.

I speculated that the various strains produced a variety of insec-ticides because they co-evolved with insects. The insects would ingest the bacterial spore with its insecticide. The toxin would kill the insect, leaving a food pouch (the dead insect) for the spore to germinate in and thrive upon.

It behooved the bacterium to co-evolve with the insects. As the insects evolved into new species, it would increase its chances of its survival through its tendency to mutate, creating many different tox-ins, one of which, hopefully, would kill the new insects. Thus, the strat-egy of this bacterium was to increase the chances that the spore would germinate in an environment (a rich food pouch) that would sustain the growth and reproduction of the organism.

This bacterium produced protein mutants that killed organisms other than insects, such as nematodes (worms)—evidence that the mi-crobe was opportunistic, seeking to co-evolve with other organisms that it could kill to perpetuate the species.

There are numerous mechanisms evolution uses to create new organisms and variations within an organism. There can be muta-tions—single changes in DNA or processes where large sections of

DNA swap positions or sexual processes—which allow huge regions and entire chromosomes to be exchanged. Viruses exist in extreme and normal environments, which lead to further shuffling of the genes of bacteria and higher organisms.

## SHUFFLING GENES BY CROSSING OVER

Plants, animals, and even yeast have more than one copy of their chromosomes, which is the genetic information needed to code for a new organism and all the genes necessary for life. Sexual reproduction gives an organism different sets of chromosomes from each parent. At the time a new organism is created, its DNA is shuffled via a process called "crossing over." In this process, the DNA is broken within one chromosome and each broken piece combines with a different chromosome.

Trillions of possible combinations exist, resulting from the way in which our mothers' and fathers' genes can cross over. These do not include mutations that might occur in an individual cell. This is why siblings are different, sometimes dramatically different, both physically and genetically. Sexual reproduction, which involves moving and mixing large regions of DNA, allows for adaptation and more rapid evolution.

## HOW DID EVOLUTION PROCEED SO QUICKLY?

Another criticism of the evolution theory concerns the supposed speed at which organisms evolve. In the previous chapter, we discussed the unlikely odds of random formation of life's essential molecules. However, once life forms existed, there was a rationale for rapid evolution.

If you've ever left food out for a few days, you might have noticed various colored blobs on it. Each of those blobs is a colony of millions of microbes that started with just a single spore or microbe on the food.

Microbes can double in number every twenty minutes or so at room temperature. On early Earth, given similar reproduction times and sufficient nutrients, in the span of several days, hundreds of billions of these initial organisms could exist in one location. Within the new organisms, thousands of mutations might have occurred.

With so many organisms involved and with such rapid reproduction, mutations quickly resulted in new life forms. Mutation rates on early Earth would have been high due to extreme conditions of heat and increased radiation. Those new life forms produced even greater numbers of organisms, which then mutated into new ones. This happened in a billion, trillion locations for a few billion years.

Mutations can be harmful, insignificant, or beneficial. When a lethal mutation or negative trait is produced, the organism rarely survives. Beneficial mutations, though rare, yield higher fitness levels and even new species with some competitive advantage, such as the bacterium that created new insecticides.

Just as having an array of tools, information, and building materials gives man the flexibility to produce computers, buildings, ships, airplanes, and all other human creations, an array of genes that evolved from early microbes resulted in all organisms. Genes produce an organism's information, cellular tools, and construction materials. The few thousand genes in bacteria can be slightly altered and utilized in different ways, resulting in a vast array of different microbes. Many of the 20,000 or so genes found in humans and animals are discovered to be strikingly similar to genes in worms, flies, and even bacteria. This illustrates how the information, tools, and construction materials produced from genes are utilized in different ways in the creation of all of nature's creatures. But many details, such as how similar genes are regulated and utilized uniquely in different organisms, are missing.

In a later chapter on consciousness, we will discuss how one gene leads to mobility in bacteria and to thoughts and memory in humans.

THE ADAPTIVE MICROBES

Another problem critics of evolution cite is the belief that humans are so much more "advanced" than the rest of the creatures on Earth. Early life, like the bacteria living on Earth today, had very limited sensory perception. They probably sensed their immediate environment—wetness or dryness, acidity, and chemicals—by their cell membranes and receptors on those membranes. They had a primitive intelligence, if intelligence is defined as responding to the environment in an opportunistic fashion, such as moving toward or away from stimuli, adapting to a lack of nutrients, and reproducing.

But bacteria and other microbes are highly evolved organisms. They have adapted to almost every environment imaginable on Earth and they have managed to live in and on every other organism. If we take "advanced" to mean an ability to adapt to the environment, microbes are actually more "advanced" than humans.

One type of bacterium, dubbed "Conan the bacterium," can withstand 3,000 times the radiation that kills a human. In other words, this bacterium would survive the radiation of an atomic blast ten times more powerful than the atomic bomb used in Hiroshima.

Microbes are the most prevalent organisms on Earth. Many bacteria exist that haven't yet been identified. Scientists are aware of them because traces of their unique RNA can be found. These unidentified microbes include bacteria living in our mouths and guts. Thus, it is likely that an even greater diversity of microbes exists and that scientists will not learn of the extent of this diversity until they learn how to identify them.

Bacterial adaptations allowed evolution leading to humans. As discussed in the beginning of this chapter, we are composite creatures, and bacteria were and are essential to our existence. Just as bacteria co-evolved with insects, they co-evolved with us. All life needs to adapt to a changing world.

LIFE MUST SENSE AND RESPOND TO THE ENVIRONMENT

Sensing and responding to the environment has been a key factor in the evolution of life. For all life, sensing one's environment and responding to those sensory signals is essential for survival. Simple single-celled organisms sensed the sun and used its energy to convert carbon dioxide and water into sugars and oxygen. This oxygen transformed Earth's atmosphere, and new forms of life utilized the oxygen and released carbon dioxide.

Eyes emerged a half billion years ago to sense light, motion, and form. Fish sensed sound waves from the movement of water along their sides. Some marine organisms and bats developed sensory capabilities for their environment, which included sonar. Birds used magnetism for guidance, and plants sensed diurnal patterns for flower production. The location of hearing for land animals developed hundreds of millions of years ago, establishing the sense of hearing near the jaw.

Cephalopods such as octopuses somehow sense their environment, rapidly changing their skins' texture, patterns, and color to create remarkable camouflage. A large portion of their brains is used for this incredible ability. Animals such as cats and dogs have a much more keen sense of smell, night vision, taste, and hearing than humans. For them, such keen senses can make the difference between life and death. Humans, on the other hand, do not necessarily need to smell urine on a fire hydrant twenty meters away.

The larger brain of humans allows more adaptation to the environment by verbal communication and rapid learning. Human brain power created computers that help us understand our world by solving complex problems, as well as a model for understanding evolution.

## CAN COMPUTERS HELP US UNDERSTAND EVOLUTION?

Digital organisms that multiply thousands of times faster than bacteria are beginning to shed light on evolution. A cluster of 200 computers at Michigan State University generate computer versions of viruses. The digital viruses can produce tens of thousands of copies of digital bits in minutes. The bits can mutate the way DNA mutates. They have not yet shown the equivalent of metabolism, but they are getting close to satisfying the checklist of characteristics of biological life.

The digital organisms evolve quite well without laboratory maintenance. They evolve toward a lifelike creature over repeated experiments. However, it is unclear what computers can teach us about the evolution of a creature as complex as man.

Scientists have much more information about and evidence for evolution than they do for the creation of the universe and the origins of life. But so far, evolution has not provided us with the answer to the great mystery: What was the first life form?

## EVOLUTION AND SPIRITUALITY

I have made the case that evolution is supported by scientific evidence. Does that mean that there is no need for spirituality and no room for it? No.

The first two chapters remind us that physicists, cosmologists, chemists, and biologists cannot explain how our universe was created or what first life was. In this chapter, I summarized how scientists utilize evolution to explain how primitive life evolved to man—that is, if first life had the basic ingredients as current life. But it is faith to assume that the first life form on Earth already had DNA or RNA similar to modern life. Suppose such faith is misplaced and first life on Earth was quite different? What if extraterrestrial life is found to posses no DNA, RNA, or protein? Scientists would scramble to develop theories as to how such life might have evolved to Earth creatures. In this case, we would still be left with the question of how first life originated.

## IS THERE A NEED AND ROOM FOR SPIRITUALITY?

Let's assume that scientists are correct and the challenge is to understand the upixels and the rules of the universe. If so, what rules have organized the upixels into life? And who wrote the rules? Was there a creator?

"Creator" could mean any one of the following:

1. A creator, godlike or not, who created our world, and then left it alone;

2. A non-god being who created life elsewhere and seeded space with primitive life;

3. A creator (supernatural or godlike) who created life on Earth or elsewhere;

4. A creator who created life, particularly humans, on Earth.

A variation of number two could lead to life evolving naturally on Earth or elsewhere. If life started elsewhere, life forms may have made it to Earth by pure chance and not by intentional seeding.

A logical person cannot rule out a creator or any other possibility. But scientists want testable theories.

## IS IT TESTABLE?

Testability, either through experiments or by observation, is a cornerstone in science. The fact that some kind of creator is consistent with all we have discussed but is not testable leads science to ignore this issue. Scientists wrestle with concepts such as the Big Bang and inflation, as well as with how to test these theories. But the big questions, such as the creation of the universe and the origin of life, are unexplained by science. This is where room for faith exists. More than that, this is where a profound need for faith exists. I have faith in science, but if spirituality can help explain our origins, I am open to such faith. Is life a miracle? How extraordinary are we?

In attempting to understand where we came from, I thought that perhaps the solution was in understanding the upixels. The upixels came out of nowhere, created our world, yielded life, and evolved into us. Since our world is made up of these mysterious upixels, what is really out there? If Wheeler is correct, then our universe can be considered mental, and mind and/or consciousness exist out there. What is reality? Is there evidence to support a mental or even spiritual universe? We've taken a look at dark energy, dark matter, and parallel universes. We've learned that 96 percent of our universe is missing. Can reality get any more bizarre?

Yes. As I will reveal, everything is energy and space; but space is not empty!

> *For my own part, I would as soon be descended from that heroic little monkey, who braved his dreaded enemy in order to save the life of his keeper; or from that old baboon, who, descending from the mountains, carried away in triumph his young comrade from a crowd of astonished dogs—as from a savage who delights to torture his enemies, offers up bloody sacrifices, practices infanticide without remorse, treats his wives like slaves, knows no decency, and is haunted by the grossest of superstitions.*

> —Charles Darwin

# WHAT IS REALITY?

# 4

# SCIENCE AND REALITY

*The only reality is mind and observations, but observations are not things. To see the universe as it really is, we must abandon our tendency to conceptualize observations as things. The universe is immaterial—mental and spiritual.*

–Richard Henry

Tommie, the nine-year-old son of a friend of mine, is excited about his new computer. He has been playing computer games since he received it. Turning to me one day, he said, "Computers are great! How does all that stuff get on the screen?"

I paused, considering my reply. "The stuff is due to individual dots called pixels. Together, they create the image."

"What are pixels?"

I explained that pixels are created by bits of energy. This energy creates the individual pixels.

Tilting his head to one side, Tommie said, "So the stuff I see is just energy."

"Not quite," I told him. "The stuff you see is created by energy."

He leaned forward on the edge of his chair. "Cool! So if I have energy, I can create the stuff on the screen?"

"Well, you need one other critical item. You need information to instruct the energy how to create the images. So, yes, with energy and the right information, all that stuff can be created."

"Then what's that box for?

"That box is the computer that transforms the energy coming from the wall through the cord. It uses information and energy to create all that stuff."

"Awesome!"

Kids ask great questions. I was glad that he didn't point to his surroundings and ask me how all that stuff was created, too, though the answer would have been the same as with the case of the computer image. All the "stuff" of our world is believed by scientists to come about through energy transformed by information! But the explanation is far more complex than the one I provided Tommie.

## JUST TWO EXCEPTIONS

At the end of the 19th century, almost everything in physics seemed to be explained—with two exceptions. One exception was the so-called ether. Ether was defined as the mysterious substance of the vacuum of space. In other words, in the 1800s, scientists thought that there was something mysterious in a vacuum—or in space, which is a near-vacuum. In those days scientists didn't possess our current understanding of atoms and matter, so we can discount such belief...Or can we?

In the early 20th century, Einstein discredited the ether concept with his theories. His theories also indicated an expanding universe which he rejected by adding a fudge factor to be consistent with a static universe—that is, a universe that always stayed the same, neither expanding nor contracting. Einstein later called this fudge factor his biggest blunder—a blunder caused by the fact that his original theory predicted a universe in motion.

In the 21st century, some scientists are reviving Einstein's fudge factor. With the appropriate adjustments in the fudge factor, they hope to explain dark energy by an anti-gravity force. But what role does dark energy play in our reality? Dark energy is believed to be 73 percent of our universe (23 percent is dark matter and the remaining four percent is the matter and energy that isn't hidden), and it is thought by scientists to explain why our universe is increasing its rate of expansion. Incredibly, though, space might also hold another kind of energy.

## SPACE AND THE VACUUM. ITS FULL OF STUFF!

In the 21st century, many scientists believe that one cannot understand the nature of the universe without considering space. Although we think of space as nearly empty, according to quantum theory, it actually is filled with enormous amounts of energy called the zero-point field. Because they lack the tools to observe or measure this energy, most physicists ignore the energy of space.

There are even transient elementary particles in space. Elementary particles, such as electrons and protons, are the components that make up atoms. These particles were misnamed because they were thought to be the smallest components of the universe. They are not. They, too, are made of upixels. And they have opposite versions of themselves. For every elementary particle such as an electron, an anti-particle exists.

For some unknown reason, anti-particles are almost never found in our world. But they can be created in particle accelerators that smash bits of matter at nearly the speed of light. When an electron and its anti-electron meet, they annihilate one another and create energy.

What is strange about space is the fact that such particles and their anti-particles are constantly being created and, by combining, are instantly destroyed. Yet the energy that created the particles and the energy released by their annihilation cannot be measured by scientists. Still, their brief existence is confirmed by experiments.

Physicist and Nobel Laureate Robert B. Laughlin states that one can infer from the results of experiments with large-particle accelerators that space is not empty, but full of "stuff." He points out that empty space and matter cooled to nearly absolute zero are similar, and that the internal motions are physically indistinguishable. In other words, when ordinary matter becomes cold enough, it acts like space. Or space acts like matter. Laughlin then said that the vacuum is like the ether that Einstein rejected: "...it [the ether] nicely captures the way most physicists actually think about the vacuum."

Several differing estimates exist for the absolute value of the energy of the vacuum. According to one calculation, empty space has more energy than all the other energy and mass in the universe—by about forty orders of magnitude which exceed the mysterious dark energy! Other scientists aren't sure how much energy exists in space. Still others believe the energy of the vacuum is the dark energy. MIT professor of physics and Nobel Laureate Frank Wilczek believes that the energy of empty spaces is "the most mysterious fact in all of physical science, the fact with the greatest potential to rock the foundations."

As surprising as learning that space and vacuums are full of energy, equally disconcerting is the fact that vacuums can exist in countless different states.

## VACUUM STATES DETERMINE WHETHER LIFE IS POSSIBLE

Vacuum states are various ways in which the vacuum can behave. Of the myriad of possible vacuum states, only very few can support life as we know it in our universe. Wait a minute, you might say. Not only is there energy in what most people consider "nothing" (a vacuum or space), but numerous forms of nothingness also exist? How can there be different vacuum states?

Scientists believe that in other universes, different properties of nature, or "laws of nature," could exist. Scientists have pondered why we have the properties of matter and energy that exist in our world. For example, suppose protons were not stable. Atoms would not be possible. Astronomer Sir Martin Rees points out that several factors, each finely tuned, are responsible for the conditions leading to life in our universe. The following factors indicate that we live in a *very* special universe:

1. The amount of hydrogen that converted to helium in the Big Bang: too little, and heavier atoms would not form; too much, and there would be no stars today.

2. The power of gravity: if gravity were weaker, stars could not form. If gravity were stronger, stars would burn out so fast there wouldn't have been time to evolve life.

3. The density of the universe: if too small, the universe would have cooled too fast. If too large, the universe would have collapsed before any life could have started.

4. The acceleration of the universe: if too small, the universe would have collapsed. If too large, the universe would have expanded too fast and frozen before life could begin.

5. Irregularities in the universe: if only a bit smaller, the universe would be too uniform to form stars. If a bit larger, the universe would have created huge stars, resulting in collapse and black holes, and no world like the one which we inhabit.

But it gets stranger. Scientists believe that different vacuum states could have different types of elementary particles and even different numbers of spatial dimensions. How many other vacuum states exist? String theorists, scientists who believe the upixels of the universe are best described as vibrating strings of energy, postulate a huge number of possible vacuum states ($10^{500}$ is one estimate: one with 500 zeroes behind it). What led to the one vacuum state that exists in our universe?

Alan Guth and David Kaiser, physicists at MIT, point out that one possible explanation is that we are part of a multiverse, in which our universe is but one of an infinite or very large number of universes. They further postulate that nothing determines the choice of vacuum for our universe. Instead, the observable universe is viewed as a tiny speck within a multiverse that consists of every possible type of vacuum. In other words, of an almost infinite number of possible ways a vacuum can behave, no one chose our own vacuum state because elsewhere in the multitude of other universes all the other possibilities also exist. This is consistent with Penrose's concept to explain inflation—discussed in Chapter 1—that our unlikely universe began as a bud on one of the trillions of branches that make up the universe.

The anthropic principle, as Guth and Kaiser define it, essentially says that there exist many possible laws of the universe, and the only reason we have the ones we have is because we are here to observe them. If the laws of the universe were such that humans or life could not exist, as possibly elsewhere in the multiverse, then no one would be able to observe and note the different laws of that universe.

Whether or not there exist other universes, string theory also postulates, through mathematical equations, that there are seven other dimensions. Why do we not see these other dimensions? One explanation is that these dimensions may exist at a realm a billion, billion times smaller than the smallest particles we can see or detect. This is about $10^{-35}$ meters in size. Although string theory is extremely complex and remains controversial, most other theories also suggest that, on this very small scale of $10^{-35}$ meters, the fundamental ingredients of our universe exist. Hence, it is the location of the upixels.

The 19th-century concept of the ether has evolved into the 21st-century concept of energy-filled space. This notion led scientists to suggest that one of the unique aspects of our universe is the vacuum state that is finely tuned in allowing life but might require seven other dimensions and a multitude of other universes having different vacuum states. This seemingly strange depiction of reality is the result of only one of two mysteries from the 1800s.

The other puzzle of the 19th century led to the question, what is matter at the most fundamental level? Most people, even non-physicist scientists, regard matter as consisting of particles. So what is there to argue about?

## "MATTER" HAS VERY PECULIAR PROPERTIES: THE QUANTUM ENIGMA

The other unsolved mystery of the 19th century was black-body radiation. When a material such as tungsten is heated enough, it emits light. But why? This mystery led to quantum theory, as well as many new enigmas and paradoxes.

Einstein taught that matter and energy are interconvertible—that is, that one can be converted to the other. In the case of the atomic bomb, a very small bit of matter was converted to an enormous amount of energy. In the case of the Big Bang, everything was inexplicably compressed to a point of energy, which upon expansion and cooling created matter and various other forms of energy. Another way of regarding matter is that it is a metaphor generated by humans to explain some aspects of energy.

In the last century, quantum theory was developed. It describes matter and energy in the same way, each having both wave and particle properties. This theory works for very small particles such as electrons and photons, but quantum effects become negligible when applied to larger objects such as billiard balls.

How can something be a wave and a particle? Although this theory is about eighty years old, experts still do not agree on its interpretation. Yet quantum theory has predicted some extremely strange things, only to have them later borne out by experiments. A wave spreads out in all directions, and it is not possible to imagine a single point where the wave exists. In like manner, quantum theory cannot give one position of an electron in a molecule, only its probability of being in various locations at any instant. However, there are finite probabilities of the electron being in quite distant locations.

## THE ULTIMATE DISAPPEARING ACT

An excellent example of the uncertainty of an electron's location was given by Michio Kaku, a physicist at the City University of New York. He described how electrons regularly dematerialize and then materialize on the other side of walls, or inside the components of PCs and CDs! He explains that what keeps two atoms locked together in a stable molecule is the fact that electrons can simultaneously be in so many places at the same time, and form an electron "cloud," which binds the atoms together; "the reason why molecules are stable and the universe does not disintegrate is that electrons can be [in] many places at the same time." But how?

## THE UPIXELS PLAY MUSICAL CHAIRS

One explanation involves the vacuum. When an electron goes to the vacuum state, it is replaced by another electron, but in a different location. The first electron went to another universe, and was replaced by an electron from another universe. This might result in a mammoth game of musical chairs where the continual replacement of one electron (or photon of light or any quantum entity) causes the movement of electrons through an infinite number of parallel universes. All these exchanges might be occurring at Planck's time scale of $1.616 \times 10^{-44}$ per second—close, but not quite simultaneous as Kaku theorized. Max Planck was the father of quantum theory, and he calculated certain constant features of the universe. Planck's time is one of these constants. Planck's length is about $10^{-35}$ meters, and this is where classical physics theories of gravity and space-time are no longer valid and quantum effects dominate. Planck's time is the time it takes to travel at the speed of light to move Planck's length.

Jeffrey Satinover, author of *The Quantum Brain*, reminds us that the great physicists Richard Feynman and John Wheeler wondered about these particles that disappear and reappear from the vacuum.

They joked that there might be only one electron in the universe:

> It is a world in which one can comfortably argue the dy-
> namics of interference among multiple universes both for-
> ward and backward in time; can ask seriously, as did Feyn-
> man and Wheeler, whether every electron in the universe
> is the same one, just reappearing through multiple loops in
> time…

This musical-chair movement of upixels through other universes would explain how an upixel can behave like both a particle and a wave, i.e. one of the hypotheses of quantum theory called "the many-worlds" version. It also would explain how particles move, since the reappearance of the upixel is in a different location.

Despite the lack of consensus as to what quantum theory actually means, without quantum mechanics we would have no lasers, television sets, computers, microwaves, CD and DVD players, mobile phones, and many other modern devices. Physicist and Nobel Prize recipient Niels Bohr stated, "Anyone who is not shocked by quantum theory has not understood it."

Decades later, Feynman, another Nobel Laureate and a former student of John Wheeler's, said the quantum world behaves like nothing with which humans have direct experience. Encouraging new students at the California Institute of Technology not to abandon quantum theory, he said:

> It is my task to convince you not to turn away because you
> do not understand it. You see my physics students don't un-
> derstand it…That is because I don't understand it. Nobody
> does.

MATTER: IT IS EVERYWHERE UNTIL WE LOOK

Imagine a jetty stopping waves in front of a harbor. Erosion produced two openings in the jetty and, as the waves pass through these openings, they radiate into the harbor. The waves in the harbor from these two openings collide and interfere with each other. In like manner, light moving through narrow slits meet and also create interference patterns.

A truly strange verification of quantum theory happens when a photon or electron passes through narrow slits (the size of a razor cut or smaller). When a single photon is aimed at a barrier with two narrow slits in it and encounters detectors behind each of the slits, the pattern appears the same as if a wave passed through both slits. This seems to defy logic. How can a single entity go through two places at once?

Quantum theory suggests that a photon, or any entity at the quantum level, takes all possible paths in going from point A to point B! This photon behaves like a wave as long as we do not measure or observe it. However, as soon as we attempt to observe it, either visually or with an instrument, the waves disappear and a photon particle appears behind one of the slits but not the other. It is as though as soon as one tries to figure out this mystery, nature makes the wave on one side disappear.

Can these phenomena be explained? Some say they are only paradoxes in a world where solids exist. But if everything is space and energy, why shouldn't energy fill space and appear to take all possible paths in going from points A to B? Scientists create metaphors of "matter" and "particle," such as photons and electrons, to explain the energy in space. But metaphor is not reality. Physicist Stephen Hawking also questions the existence of particles: "Maybe there are no particle positions and velocities, but only waves. It is just that we try to fit the waves to our preconceived ideas."

The bias that "particles" should not take all possible paths, whereas waves would from point A to point B, is based on the billiard-ball paradigm of solids comprising the world. Reality may be that there are no solid particles, only energy waves filling space.

## WHAT IF I CHANGE MY MIND?

Suppose I put devices in front of the slits that can mark a photon (the details of the marking are not important here). In that case, the marking of the photon is an observation and results in the photon behaving as a particle, not a wave, and being detected behind only one slit. Now suppose I design the experiment to mark the photon in front of the slits, but *before* the photon hits the detector, I change my mind and do not mark the photon. The result is the photon behaving as a wave! This implies that consciousness creates reality—the explanation of quantum theory that Wheeler supports.

The quantum world has confounded the greatest minds in science for eight decades. There is no agreed-upon explanation of these phenomena. And there is another aspect to the quantum world that Einstein called "spooky."

## NONLOCALITY: INSTANT COMMUNICATION OR UPIXEL TELEPATHY?

Particles at the quantum level can communicate instantly—faster than the speed of light. This effect, called nonlocality, has been demonstrated with particles at great distances. As we've discussed, particles at the quantum level exist in a probabilistic state, having all possible states. But when they interact, each "knows" the other's quantum state and instantly matches its properties, regardless of distance.

Here is a fictitious example. Frank and Pete are casino owners, who own gaming establishments in Las Vegas, Atlantic City, and Monte Carlo. Their vigilance in looking out for cheating schemes includes employing the world's best security firms. Frank learns of a spooky phenomenon and phones Pete. He says that if one were to allow two slot machines to touch and then move them apart, the two machines would both have the same results at the same time. If one machine gave a cherry, a bar, and a seven, the other slot would also give a cherry, a bar, and a seven. This would only happen if the machines were not exposed to any other slot machines. Pete thinks that Frank has finally lost his mind.

Frank wants to meet Pete outside of Vegas, with each of them bringing a slot machine. Frank bets Pete twenty big ones that he is right. Pete likes easy money and thinks that Frank is drunk. They meet in the desert, each with a slot machine in the back of his SUV. Pete touches his slot machine with Frank's, and then moves it back into his SUV.

"That's it?" Pete asks.

"Yep."

Pete drives ten miles down the road and plugs his slot into an electrical outlet at his house. Frank also goes home. They talk by cell phone. At the same time, they pull the levers, and both slots come up bar, seven, seven. "You owe me twenty grand, Pete." Pete says no way, doubles the bet, and insists that he fly a slot from Atlantic City to repeat the exercise. He does this, and both machines give seven, bar, seven. Pete again doubles the bet and flies a slot from Monte Carlo, has it touch Frank's slot, and then flies it to Colorado for the test. Both slots give cherry, bar, seven, both winners betrayed by the musical ringing of both machines. Pete has just lost $80,000. Frank says, "Hey, Pete, cheer up. You just won four quarters."

Although this weird "telepathy" does not actually happen with slot machines, it does happen with upixels, illustrating the strangeness that exists at quantum dimensions. When upixel "particles" such as photons interact, they become entangled. Even when the photons move away, measurement of the spin of one photon causes the other photon to instantly take on a predictable spin value. Spin is a property that quantum particles have akin to the spin of a top. In experiments during which scientists allow photons to interact (entangle), they synchronize their properties. The following example, unlike the slot-machine story, is a summary of actual experiments.

Imagine a top spinning at an angle relative to the ground. It could have any number of angles relative to the ground. Now, imagine that you place two spinning "quantum tops," photons, in a fiber-optic cable. They become entangled. They must be "shielded" from other photons or they will also entangle with them. Each photon has all possible spinning states. Then, they move away from each other. When you observe the spin state of one of the photons, you "freeze" one of its spin states into reality. The fact that this one spin state has been observed by you is instantly communicated to the other photon. The other photon now has the opposite spin state. With photons, this has been demonstrated even though the photons were moved three kilometers apart in an optical fiber.

The potential utility of nonlocality is awesome—scientists are attempting to create quantum computers using this amazing feature of upixels. But how do they explain this "upixel telepathy?" What type of connections allows these upixels to communicate instantly?

The nonlocality feature of quantum theory spawns suggestions from physicists that information passes through hidden variables, other dimensions, or other universes. These are startling possibilities. Since the upixels are the basic constituents of the universe, can action on one upixel be "felt" by all the upixels in the universe? If so, one might regard the universe as alive.

### WHOLENESS

Nonlocality implies wholeness. In simple terms, the universe must then be seen as a whole. Since upixels have instant communication, our actions and the actions of others affect the entire universe. Consider a vast ocean. You can study a cup of its water, its lagoons, or its tides, but this will not reveal the whole. The flick of a fin of a small fish changes the motion of water molecules around it and, as the ripple spreads, minute molecular interactions impact the entire ocean. Quantum mechanics implies the same sort of interactions. But in the case of upixels, the effect is instantaneous. David Bohm, a world-class physicist, stated "the concepts of relativity theory and quantum theory directly contradict each other." He continues to say that a new theory is needed and the "best place to begin is what [the two theories] have in common. This is undivided wholeness." In other words, we are one with each other and we are one with the universe—another concept consistent with many religions and spiritual teachings. The Brahman of the Hindus is the cosmic web of the interconnected universe. Mahayana Buddhism's *Avaatamsaka Sutra* describes the world as a network of mutual relations in which all events and things interact with each other in an infinitely complex manner.

The Dalai Lama, during his studies of quantum theory, visited David Bohm and other quantum physicists. His Buddhist views reflect Bohm's quantum perspective:

> ...any belief in an objective reality grounded in the assumption of intrinsic, independent existence is untenable...[to possess such existence] would imply that things and events are somehow complete unto themselves and therefore entirely self-contained. This would mean that nothing has the capacity to interact with and exert influence on other phenomena...In our naïve or commonsense view of the world, we relate to things and events as if they possess an enduring intrinsic reality.

So, how does one study the universe in its entirety? Wholeness makes it obvious that studying a quantum effect of an atom or upixel without also considering all the other constituents of the universe will result in observing merely an aspect of reality. How do we include all the things in the universe we can see, parallel universes, other hidden dimensions, dark matter, dark energy, and the energy of the vacuum? One can regard all of these as missing information.

INFORMATION TRANSFORMS ENERGY INTO REALITY

What are the rules that transform the upixels of the universe into matter, energy, time, gravity, motion, and our reality? What rules led to the upixels resulting in our world? This is what Einstein searched for until his death.

Einstein sought what can be regarded as information. Thus, one view of reality is that everything is only energy transformed by information. Obviously, information is not material. But how can there be information without consciousness? It is perhaps more like the "spirit" which some individuals believe manifests itself in life.

Everything is energy and information; consciousness must exist to create reality. I call the stuff of our world upixels. The great 20th-century scientist Sir Arthur Eddington deemed it as such: "To put the conclusion crudely—the stuff of the world is mind-stuff."

This view has become more prevalent in the 21st century, as shown by physicist and astronomer Richard Henry, who was quoted in the beginning of this chapter as saying: "The universe is immaterial—mental and spiritual."

## A 21ST-CENTURY PERSPECTIVE: UPIXELS' COMPUTATIONS RESULT IN OUR WORLD

Seth Lloyd of MIT and Jack Ng of the University of North Carolina, leading scientists in quantum-information theory and quantum-gravity theory, stated in 2004 that the universe is the ultimate computer, having performed $10^{123}$ operations so far. They said that "...the universe is computing itself." How can this happen?

All interactions between the upixels convey information. Thus, upixels compute upon collision. The upixels are computing their own dynamic evolution. They evolved into our world. Is there such a "universal" computer program? But if upixels' own computations resulted in our reality, what is the computer program giving the information?

No one has shown what program, information, or rule transforms upixels into our reality. "Information" is a metaphor to describe an element of our reality. What are other possibilities of reality? Perhaps we are not "seeing" the whole picture.

## OR, YOU CAN CHOOSE A PLATO METAPHOR

Physicist Stephen Webb, from the Open University in England, describes Plato's *Allegory of the Cave*, where prisoners only view a two-dimensional world of shadows. Webb points out that, had physicists been among these prisoners, they might have developed theories on how objects move and interact in such a two-dimensional world. It would have been difficult or impossible for anyone in that world to comprehend that a three-dimensional world exists.

In our three-dimensional world, are we merely viewing shadows of a higher-dimensional world? Numerous metaphors of science explain that there are, or could be, other dimensions, universes, or worlds beyond our comprehension, but how do other dimensions or universes explain the manner in which upixels become our realities?

Twenty-first-century theories of what is out there—space, information, other universes, other dimensions, and upixels—are like elements of a collage that create our reality. Some of these elements exist in realms inaccessible to us. I use the word "realms," but like Russian Matrioshka dolls, they are all nested aspects of the same reality and inaccessible to our perceptions. I will elaborate on this in the next section. In our universe, only when some of the upixels agglomerate to larger-sized entities do we notice "matter."

## REALMS OF REALITY

There are four realms of reality. But like the nested Russian dolls, we can see only the larger aspects of our world. The first is information. It is here that information is available instantly, thus allowing nonlocality, the phenomenon where information can be transmitted instantly. Here the information of everything that was, is, and ever will be, exists. The rules of the universe then transform the information into the other realms of reality, and it is at these next realms that one finds the upixels. Can information exist without consciousness? We will explore in Chapter 7 the manner in which consciousness/mind resides in this information realm.

The second realm of reality is the vacuum state, having quantum particles such as electrons, light, and other quantum entities constantly appearing from one universe and moving to another. Earlier, we discussed this feature of quantum stuff popping out of one place and instantly reappearing elsewhere as a characteristic of the vacuum of space. The energy of the vacuum resides here. Other universes might be accessible from this realm of reality.

The third realm is at quantum dimensions—about $10^{-35}$ meters. Here we have a nexus of the quantum world, space, and other dimensions. As one examines smaller volumes of space, at $10^{-35}$ meters, quantum fluctuations become a roaring tumult. The upixels appear in this third realm, coming from the vacuum and other universes. Here, the electrons, light particles, and other quantum entities enter our world and agglomerate into larger "objects" that become our realities. But how?

At first glance of a wave on the ocean, it appears that the same water molecules stay with the wave as it moves, giving the illusion that the same water molecules are moving. Upon careful observation, we find that at every instant of time water molecules move in and out of the wave. In like fashion, the upixels that make up our world zip in and out of the "ocean" of the vacuum and other universes to be in our universe for an instant and help create the illusion of motion.

Suppose the upixels are exchanged many trillion times or more per second. That would give the appearance of motion of the upixels. In reality, however, the individual upixels that make up our perceptions of motion are different each moment.

We will get to the fourth realm soon. First, let's discuss this important point of how the upixels appear from the vacuum.

## THE UPIXELS ZIP IN AND OUT OF OUR WORLD

The electrons and all quantum-level entities are constantly zipping in and out of existence via the vacuum, parallel universes, or other dimensions. We have no way of recognizing that this is happening, and assume that the quantum entities are the same and moving.

We, along with everything in our solar system, appear to be moving around the galaxy at about 570,000 miles per hour, and the universe appears to be expanding at many times that rate. Therefore, in space, we and our surroundings appear to be moving at over a million miles per hour. However, we and everything in the universe are composed of upixels that zip in and out of existence at ten million, trillion, trillion, trillion times per second (or, at Planck's time, $5.391 \times 10^{44}$ per second). The musical-chair movement of upixels is an alternative explanation of motion, and it can be consistent with parallel universes or other dimensions of string theory.

Imagine placing a penny on the ground. Now, place another penny next to it and remove the original penny. This is akin to the process I described above. Instead of pennies, there is an upixel that disappears and is replaced by another upixel the width of an upixel ($1.616 \times 10^{-35}$ meters—Planck's distance) away from the original upixel. Now imagine in one second this happens $5.391 \times 10^{44}$ times. In one second the upixel appears to move 299,792 kilometers—exactly the speed of light! Yet, the upixel was replaced $5.391 \times 10^{44}$ times. How many times is that? In one second, the upixel would be replaced a thousand times more than the number of protons lying side by side, for the eighty billion trillion miles that light traveled since the Big Bang.

This means that the stuff in you, me, and our surroundings is changing at this incredible rate. Somehow, we manage to exist, be conscious, and feel.

## FINALLY, THE WORLD WE EXPERIENCE: THE FOURTH REALM

Reality is all of the realms: the realm of information, the realm of the vacuum, the realm of the quantum and upixels, and, finally, the fourth realm. In this realm the quantum particles combine to yield matter as we know and observe it. Then, what are we? We are all of the above. In one realm, we are but information. All of the happenings of all our lives are recorded in this realm of reality. In another realm, we are energy. This energy is an essential aspect of our being that we have yet to fully understand and appreciate.

Table 3. A Speculative Description of the Realms of Reality

| Realm of reality | Comments |
|---|---|
| Information | All the information that ever was, is, and ever will be for our universe, and all other universes. |
| Vacuum and (virtual) energy | Access to other universes. |
| Quantum, about $10^{-35}$ meters | This is the nexus to the vacuum and other dimensions. The upixels and quantum particles move to the vacuum realm and are instantly replaced by an identical particle, but at a different location. |
| Atomic—about $10^{-18}$ meters and larger | Most of our perceived reality. Upixels become elementary particles. |

It is as though scientists have been using a crude digital camera to photograph our world. As they enlarge the image to decipher reality, the picture first becomes grainy and then only an abstract image with scattered pixels. The vast space between the grains contains the other 96 percent of our world; the current cameras and an arsenal of scientific tools have not filled in the blanks. The picture of reality will remain transcendent until we fully understand what is missing. And this world that we are attempting to visualize might be a mere speck in an infinite universe.

## OR, YOU CAN WAIT FOR THE NEXT THEORY

For those who attempt to understand the current metaphors of science—which include parallel universes, missing dark matter and energy, information transforming energy into matter, energy in space, energy strings, and other dimensions—all of this might seem like bad science fiction. Author Douglas Adams wrote in *The Restaurant at the End of the Universe*:

> There is a theory which states that if ever anybody discovers exactly what the universe is for and why it is here, it will instantly disappear and be replaced by something even more bizarre and inexplicable. There is another theory which states that this has already happened.

## THE NEW SCIENTIFIC TRUTH IS AN OLD SPIRITUAL TRUTH

In the 16th century, Copernicus demonstrated that the sun did not revolve around the Earth. This was the beginning of the modern scientific era. Early in the 20th century, quantum theory led to transcendence beyond materialism and even language. With 21st-century revelations, we are at the dawn of a new truth, which merges concepts of science and spirituality. This new truth will radically alter our worldview: We are one with our world, and this oneness, information, mind, and consciousness, is the universe and us.

Our reality is created by energy transformed by information. The universe is mental and spiritual, just as spirituality teaches. This realization is a giant step towards healing the rift between science and spirituality. For thousands of years, the East Indians and Chinese taught that everything was energy. Many Eastern religions also contend that life is an illusion.

Is there a scientific explanation for this illusion? If matter is immaterial, what is it that we see and experience? What information is carried by the dark energy and the energy of the vacuum? We humans have based our reality on only 4 percent of what is "out there." In the next chapter, I will show how we perceive (or misperceive) only a billionth of that 4 percent!

> *When he speaks of "reality" the layman usually means something obvious and well-known, whereas it seems to me that precisely the most important and extremely difficult task of our time is to work on elaborating a new idea of reality. This is also what I mean when I always emphasize that science and religion must be related in some way.*
>
> –Wolfgang Pauli

# 5
# MISPERCEPTIONS

*Reality is not only stranger than we suppose but stranger than we can suppose.*

–J.B.S. Haldane

My brothers, sisters, and I regularly visited our parents for Thanksgiving. My mother always looked forward to our visits and prepared food days in advance. On the street outside of my parents' house, I would detect the delectable aromas of roast turkey, potatoes, pies, and an assortment of other foods.

We would all sit down to eat, except for my mother, who hovered about us and searched for a bare spot on a plate to bombard with food. Even the newcomers to the family, my siblings' wives and husbands, quickly learned the "Kim maneuver" of shielding their plates with their hands at lightning speed lest another helping of something would descend. Sometimes, though, they would fail to notice my mother, armed with a new dish in one hand and a ladle in the other. Usually the food would make the plate, but sometimes it would be a tie, with the food on top of the hands.

We would retreat to walk off a calorie or two and avoid the onslaught of hundreds more. Outside, red, yellow, and brown leaves skittered in the cool, crisp air.

Upon our return, large dinner plates, each loaded with generous portions of several desserts, would adorn the table. My mother would then say, "You didn't finish. Sit and have a bite more."

## THE ULTIMATE MIRAGE

Human reality is an illusion, an incomplete representation of our world. But how could all that our senses and intellects record be a mirage? If everything is energy, what are we experiencing? The sight of my family around me, the feel of the chair, the sound of conversations, the aromas and tastes of the food—how do all of those things come about from energy transformed by information?

As I investigated scientific theories as to where we came from and what we are, I realized that those questions were the equivalent of asking: what is reality? Reality is what really exists "out there." The upixels are somehow transformed into our reality. I know that I experienced Thanksgiving dinner, but what was really there? Several Eastern religions teach that life is an illusion, but what is the explanation?

The great mystery of reality is how space and energy become all we experience. Part of the answer lies in the "tricks" our brains play on us in representing reality.

Suppose we look at ourselves. What we see is what we are, right? Wrong. Let's go back to our fundamental knowledge of atoms, the basic building blocks that make up all molecules.

The brain's representations are simplified constructions of an extremely complex world that allow us to function in that world. The first step in attempting to understand reality is to realize that our perceptions are incomplete.

## A QUICK LESSON ON THE DIMENSIONS OF AN ATOM

When I first studied chemistry, I learned that atoms are made up of electrons orbiting a nucleus, which is made up of protons and neutrons. The models in my high school class portrayed the atom as approximately the size of a basketball with the center, representing the nucleus, the size of a baseball. Orbiting the baseball-sized nucleus, about six inches away, were electrons about the size of marbles.

Using accurate proportions, I will make the nucleus a foot in diameter. The protons and neutrons occupy space about an inch in diameter. Small subatomic particles, when confined at the temperatures we experience, are quite active. Thus, the protons and the neutrons in the nucleus are zipping about each other at 40,000 miles per second.

Now, run a marathon, because the electrons at any instant would probably be about 26 miles away, probably popping in and out of existence in different directions at nearly the speed of light. Why use the word "probably" twice in the last sentence? Because the electrons only have certain probabilities of being at given locations, and they have no dimensions—hence, they're invisible.

Earlier, we discussed how electrons seem to be in many places at the same time. This feature holds molecules together. Only one-trillionth of the volume of an atom is the nucleus: the rest is space. But even the nucleus itself is only space with a bit of energy in it. Thus, atoms and molecules are space and energy. We do not really see us. Everything is space with energy in it. Energy is without dimension, so the brain simplifies a complex reality.

You might say, so what? Perhaps what our eyes see is the bit of matter that isn't space. Not so.

## TRICKS OUR BRAINS PLAY

To illustrate our brains' attempts to make sense of what is out there, William Tiller and Walter Dibble, material scientists from Stanford University, described experiments in which individuals put on "upside-down glasses" that made everything appear upturned. This inverted world was what they saw until about two weeks later, when their brains turned the images right side up again, even though the subjects were still wearing the glasses. Tiller and Dibble reported that, when the subjects removed the glasses, they saw an upside-down world for about two weeks before the images returned to normal.

This is a clear demonstration that what we see is not reality. Vision is an attempt by our brains to make sense of what is seen even if it turns the world upside down. But what about all the other times when upside-down glasses aren't being worn? What do we see?

## WE EVOLVED TO SEE FALSE IMAGES

Light is a form of energy that can have various frequencies. The frequency is the rate at which the energy or light vibrates or oscillates as it travels. Photons have a huge range of possible frequencies, and only about a billionth of these frequencies are visible to us as light. When I look at an object, what I "see" are photons (light) that have reflected off the object's molecules into my eyes. If molecules are space with a bit of energy in it, how does the light become reflected?

Light is reflected when its interaction with the atoms' or molecules' energy slows it down. You see reflected light when clear glass is held at an angle to a light source. This is vividly illustrated during driving, when sunlight strikes windshields at the right angle. The glare can be blinding. The light is slowed down by interaction with the energy of the glass molecules, and it "swerves" at the reflected angle. This is somewhat like one half of a car traveling on paved road, while the opposite half is on gravel. The interaction of the tires with the gravel slows down the car on that side while the tires on the other side are not slowed. In this case, the car will swerve toward the gravel.

You see no reflected light when you hold a clear glass directly between you and the light. The light passes through it, and all you see is bright light. This would be like driving a car on the pavement and then shifting to a gravel road. As the front tires of the car interact with the gravel at the same time, the car does not swerve, but it does slow down.

Physicist and astronomer Sir Arthur Eddington, when speaking of the atom, said, "It is 'really' empty space." What I saw at Thanksgiving were photons interacting with energy and swerving into my eyes.

What is color, then?

## COLOR—DOES IT REALLY EXIST?

Was the pumpkin that Thanksgiving really made up of "orange" molecules or "orange" energy? There is no actual color. Light has no color. Color is an illusion. It is simply a way in which the brain processes the different frequencies of visible light as it enters our eyes. In somewhat the same way we color a map to make it more understandable, the brain represents the information it receives as various colors.

How does this process take place? Visible light is a mixture of various frequencies. Visible light is absorbed if the light strikes electrons in atoms or molecules that possess the same vibrational frequency. The frequencies not absorbed are reflected. The eyes receive these frequencies of light, and the brain calculates which were absorbed and "paints in" the color. If all of the visible light is absorbed, the brain paints that area black.

Eyes process the photons that have reflected into them and transfer the information to the brain. The brain then processes the information into an image, which we feel is a true representation of what we see. Stated another way, light that reaches our eyes simply supplies information to our brains as to what types of energy it has interacted with. Our brains process the information that the light energy supplies and give us representations of the energy as material objects, such as buildings and rocks, earth and stars—everything in the universe.

In the last chapter, we discussed how physicists believe the universe is energy transformed by information. The brain somehow transforms a minuscule percentage of the available energy into information that is understandable. In doing so, it simplifies the energy/information reality. Psychologist Robert Ornstein states in his book, *Multimind*: "Our world appears to us the way it does, because we are built the way we are, not because of how the world is."

Think of the brain and eyes as marvelous instruments capable of capturing a narrow spectrum of light and creating images, which, although not representative of what is really out there, help us function in the world.

I mentioned that there are various forms of light—also called electromagnetic radiation. Humans and most animals evolved to detect the segment of the spectrum we call visible light. It is interesting to imagine that, if we had the appropriate apparatus to receive and process other forms of electromagnetic radiation in our physical makeup, we could receive and interpret radio, television, and cellphone messages directly—without electrical devices!

## BACK TO EMPTY SPACE

If everything is mainly space, how is it that we feel objects and do not fall through a chair when we sit on it? The answer is that all atoms have electrons buzzing about a nucleus and all electrons are negatively charged. Remember, the electrons seem to be everywhere at once. The repulsion of electrons prevents us from falling through a chair, even though both chairs and humans are essentially space with a smattering of energy. Like charges repel, and this repulsion is felt by our skin and transmitted to our brains. This contributes to the illusion that an object is solid and that the world is filled with solid objects. Our deception is reinforced by two of our senses, sight and touch.

Billiard balls bounce off of each other and add to the deception, we hear the cracking sound the balls make as they strike each other. The bounce is due to electronic repulsion. This creates sound waves. The sound waves are movement of air: a narrow range of the energy from such movement is translated into information by our ears and sent to the brain.

Not only can matter be felt, it can be heavy. If matter is but energy, why is a boulder heavy? Weight is caused by gravity acting on mass, and all matter has mass. But what is mass? Nobel Laureate Frank Wilczek explains that the mass of "normal" matter (as opposed to dark matter) is simply due to the movement of upixels in the nucleus (99.9 percent of the mass) and the movement of electrons (0.1 percent). As I explained in the last chapter, such movement is consistent with the musical-chair exchange of upixels zipping in and out of our universe. We are merely space and energy, thus it should not be surprising that some forms of space and energy (the boulder, for example) are not affected by our feeble attempts.

What we see, feel, and hear are therefore creations of our brains, enabling us to make sense of our world.

## TIME——ANOTHER ILLUSION

What about our sense of time? Is time also an illusion? Yes.

We seem to live by the clock. Time defines what we do and when we do it. Yet physicists cannot define time without describing it relative to space. Therefore, another illusion we have is that time is the same for everyone. This is not true.

Every time we travel, our aging, relative to others who are not traveling, is different. At the speeds we travel, the difference is extremely small, but real. We all have our own senses of time, our own clocks. When we see someone, we think it is in real time, but it takes time for the light to reach us and for our brains to process the data. By the time we have an image, the person, in reality, would have already changed.

Suppose scientists develop an instrument to detect a planet 50,000 light years away. What we would observe is the way the planet was 50,000 ago. Suppose, too, that simultaneous with our observation of this planet, someone on that planet was observing Earth. That entity would not see us, nor any evidence of us, for what it would observe is the Earth of 50,000 years ago. Therefore, both of us could exist at the "same time," but be incapable of seeing or communicating with each other. We wouldn't even know of each other's existence. The thirteen-billion-year-old galaxies that cosmologists observe are the oldest fossils in the universe. But they are illusions. Most of these galaxies' stars have long ago burned out, and the remnants have moved trillions of miles during the time their light traveled to us. Or have they?

Of all our misconceptions, the concept that is the most difficult to grasp is that time itself is phantasm.

## WHAT TIME IS IT?

Einstein said, "For we convinced physicists, the distinction between past, present, and future is only an illusion, however, persistent." Physicist and author Brian Greene interprets Einstein's quotation by explaining that past, present, and future all exist in space-time:

> They eternally occupy their particular point in space-time. There is no flow. If you were having a great time at the stroke of midnight on New Year's Eve 1999, you still are, since that is just one immutable location in space-time.

How can every moment of each of our lives be somewhere out there in space-time? It gets more bizarre. Many scientists believe that we live in an infinite universe, and that all possible events could also be out there in space-time. This seems like a fantastic statement. I will explain why scientists are making this claim over the next few pages. But if all possible events exist "out there," why not our being in heaven or reliving our lives? Can this be a rationale for an afterlife? If so, this theory could help heal the rift between science and spirituality. Let's explore this theory further.

You'll recall that, in the last chapter, I described the upixels as zipping in and out of our universe $10^{44}$ times per second to and from parallel universes. I also illustrated how subatomic matter behaves like a particle when observed and a wave when not. Let me explain this "many worlds" theory, using the wave-particle conundrum of the double-slit experiment as an example.

A scientist ponders when to set up an experiment—today or tomorrow. She decides today, thereby accessing one of the numerous possibilities that reside in the information realm discussed in the last chapter. Information for our universe and parallel universes are accessed from the vacuum. The possibility of delaying the experiment remains in another universe and, in that world, she does the experiment the next day. Today in our universe, she places detectors in front of both slits to observe the photon. Her decision to use detectors results in the observation of a particle behind one of the slits. In another universe the particle appears behind the other slit. The possibility of her not using detectors would result in a wave and resides in yet another universe.

The many worlds explanation of quantum theory was discussed in the last chapter. One of its assertions is that *every possible combination of upixels* exists in an *infinite number of parallel universes*. Why do we not perceive these other universes? Do many scientists really believe in this seemingly strange theory?

Numerous physicists subscribe to the concept of multiple or parallel universes. Nobel Laureate Steven Weinberg uses a radio analogy. Our surroundings are filled with radio waves and other frequencies of light. However, with our radios we can tune in to only one of these at a time. While we are tuned into one frequency, the other frequencies cannot be accessed. In like manner, we are "tuned in" to only our universe. Physicist Michio Kaku explains the parallel universes' relationship to our world:

> And because each world consists of trillions upon trillions of atoms, this means that the energy differences can be quite large…this means that the waves of each world vibrate at different frequencies and cannot interact anymore. For all intents and purposes, the waves of these various worlds do not interact or influence [our world or] each other.

Because these worlds do not interact or influence each other, they could be occupying the same space as our universe! These other worlds or universes alongside ours provide a possible explanation of why space is filled with enormous energy. But can scientists prove any of this?

Scientists postulate multiple or parallel universes to explain the slippery concepts of science, such as the quantum paradox and the space-time conundrum of all possible events existing out there. Ironically, in their attempt to find a non-spiritual solution to these mysteries, scientists propose theories that might be impossible to test or verify, thereby embracing what some might call faith. Science prides itself in having explanations that are verifiable, either through experimentation or by predicting future observations. Yet, it is unclear if multiple or parallel universes can ever be verified.

Not all scientists subscribe to the notion of parallel universes, however. Physicist Robert B. Laughlin cautions scientists against resorting to theories that cannot be tested and compares this type of "theory" to accepting mythology:

> We have really unfalsifiable concepts of budding little baby universes with different properties...Beyond even that we have the anthropic principle—the "explanation" that the universe we can see has the properties it does by virtue of our being in it.

Critics notwithstanding, many scientists believe that past, present, future, and every possible event are out there in space-time. As I pondered this, I realized that if this assertion is true, the "time" of the Big Bang and all "times" are now. We are not conscious of these other worlds, "past" events, and the "future" because, as Weinberg states, we are not tuned in to them.

## MORE EVIDENCE OF THE SPIRITUAL

In the last chapter I explained that physicists believe that we live in a mental and spiritual universe. This spiritual universe contains all times with no interval between events.

Other than the wave/particle dilemma and speculation of parallel universes, is there any evidence supporting that all "times" exist out there? Yes. Quantum entanglement was discussed in the last chapter. Upixels, when entangled, can communicate information, instantly supporting the notion of an information realm in which all of the past, present, and future reside. What is the possible explanation for entanglement? A fifth dimension of space, which could be at a dimension too small for humans to observe. This realm and entanglement have spiritual implications. In his book *The God Effect,* science writer Brain Clegg likens entanglement to a God-like phenomenon. Physicist Vlatko Vedral of Imperial College London suggests a link between entanglement and life: "So, might it be not only that quantum effects are responsible for the behavior of inanimate matter, but that the magic of entanglement is also crucial in the existence of life?"

Why doesn't entanglement of all upixels spread instantly through the universe? Roger Penrose suggests that observations from life stop it—for example, when a light wave is observed, it collapses to a particle—at least in our universe, where an observer detects the light and assumes that events are sequential.

Brian Josephson, the Nobel Laureate for physics in 2001, suggested that entanglement provides a mechanism to explain telepathy: "These developments [entanglement] may lead to an explanation of processes still not understood within conventional science such as telepathy."

Can it be that those who experience ESP or contact with the dead do tune in to these realms of the universe not available to most of us? Our misperception of time could be inhibiting the majority of us. We will discuss further the relationship of entanglement, life, and mind in later chapters.

Is our consciousness limited to just the present and past? If the past and future are out there, why does time appear to flow chronologically?

Time appears to flow in our universe only in one direction. We see a glass drop and break, but we never see a heap of broken glass leap up onto a table and form a glass. This is due to one of the laws of science.

Let me explain this law of order evolving to disorder with an example.

## FELINE DISTEMPER

Imagine you are writing a book and modifying the manuscript every few weeks. You have eighty versions of the loose-leaf manuscript sitting on a bookshelf. You failed to save the last several versions on your computer. Your cats came in and knocked over the bookshelf, spilling the pages onto the floor in a random heap. They attacked the pile with relish, enjoying the game of shuffling the pages. After denigrating words and gestures to your cats, you picked up the mess and threw it into a few large boxes. You then headed for the local pub to drown your sorrows. Disorder occurred. The pages and manuscripts were scrambled. When you returned home, you found the cats had discovered the boxes, knocked them over again, and continued their game.

Suppose you are an animal lover and decide to keep your cats anyway. Each time you box the papers, the cats repeat their game, resulting in additional disorder. You and your cats will not live long enough to repeat this exercise enough times to get the manuscripts and their pages in the correct order. So if the manuscripts need to be sorted, do not rely on your cats. In our world, everything tends to move to more disorder, because we started in a rare state of extreme order. But why? If all events are out there, what is going on?

We *believe* time is moving from present to future. This is merely our perception of our universe evolving to greater disorder. Time *appears* to flow because somehow the information of a particular moment acts on the upixels. In our universe, the upixels appear to evolve to greater disorder. This is why you see ice melt in a glass of water and never see a glass of water form an ice cube. Perceived disorder projects into our consciousness as time. As the upixels appear more disordered, we perceive the passage of time. However, scientists believe that the past and future exist beyond our perception. So with all the reality out there to choose from, the brain needs to simplify an extremely complex world. If we could verify this by accessing the past and the future, will this help us heal the rift between science and spirituality? We will continue this discussion in later chapters.

Is science's concept of time new? The ancient Eastern religions describe in their writings higher states of consciousness involving an experience of space and time similar to the teachings of modern physics. The Taoists and the Buddhists speak of awareness as an infinite, timeless, and dynamic present. Interestingly, both this spiritual perspective and the existence of parallel universes are unfalsifiable.

As strange as our misperception of the world seems, it gets stranger.

## WE ARE A SHADOW OF OUR FORMER SELVES: WHICH ONE IS US?

Sight, touch, sound, and time are illusions, but what about our bodies? It is said that one can never wade into the same river due to the fact that the component water molecules are constantly changing. Similarly, the molecules within us are continually changing, too.

As I stated earlier, scientists believe that the elements within us came from stars. Additionally, nearly all of the elements currently in our bodies were not there a few years ago. We are made up of about 70 percent water and about 30 percent solid components (including bone, muscle, and protein). The vast majority of the molecules in our bodies (water) is constantly being eliminated and replaced with the water we drink.

Some of that water now in us came from comets and meteors. The other molecules, such as sugars, carbohydrates, fats, proteins, and even the components of bone are also constantly being replaced. Tens of billions of our cells—our skin and gut lining—die daily and are replaced with new cells. Atoms and molecules have been flowing through our bodies since we were born. The average lifespan of any atom or molecule residing within us is only a few weeks or so. The body continually takes in new atoms and molecules and flushes out the older components.

Even DNA is being repaired and synthesized. If we are a collection of atoms arranged in molecules, then which atoms make up and explain us? There are the atoms of last year, last month, last week, and yesterday.

## WE CONTINUALLY MELT INTO THE WORLD: WHAT KEEPS US CONSISTENT?

Atoms that once were in us might now be in other humans, in plants, or in the ocean. What is certain is that they are dispersed far and wide. Consider the carbon and oxygen that were consumed by us as sugars and carbohydrates. Much of those sugars and carbohydrates were converted to energy and expelled as carbon dioxide from our lungs.

Of course, the carbon dioxide we expel could then become a carbonate mineral (rock), or be taken up by plants and converted to biomass, and later could be eaten by animals and eventually consumed by a human. Over time a single water molecule may originate in a distant galaxy, become part of a comet, part of the Earth's early ocean, pass through countless organisms, and spend only minutes in us before returning to the environment. How can this happen if all events are "out there" at once?

The important point is that all of the atoms in our bodies are one with the environment. We are just a collection of atoms formed into molecules, cells, tissues, and organs in a body. However, all of these atoms and molecules appear to be constantly moving in and out of us when, in reality, it is the upixels moving through other dimensions or universes that result in this illusion. We have the perception of being the same person, yet we are not. The upixels that comprise us and everything in the universe are jumping in and out of existence, and even in and out of parallel universes.

Many leading scientists employ various metaphors, such as added dimensions and/or parallel universes. If we are incapable of perceiving the vast majority of what is before us—let alone the infinite universe, other dimensions, and parallel universes—it is entirely possible that we may never realize or even grasp the complete concept of reality.

## SPIRITUALITY TEACHES: IIMPORTANT PARTS OF OUR WORLD ARE HIDDEN

An increasing number of physicists in the last several decades have demonstrated a willingness to break ranks and think outside the box. With their new metaphors of parallel universes and upixels jumping in and out of existence, they are arriving at the conclusion that we live in a spiritual universe of mind and energy waves. All of this verifies the concept of wholeness. We are all intricately connected with each other and the universe—another concept taught by Eastern religions. The upixels are connected via nonlocality. Upixels that make up molecules shuffle through the cosmos, humans, and our environment. Thus, the metaphors of "matter" and "atoms" present difficulties in explaining reality, life, and what gives humans their existence. We have seen that it is mind and consciousness that convert the upixels into our reality, but how?

## HOW DO WE MAKE SENSE OUT OF MISPERCEPTIONS?

Humans have incomplete perceptions. A minuscule amount of information, relative to what is out there, is processed and mapped in the brain. Missing most of what is "out there," people are biased by the limited input they take in, process, and comprehend.

We live in a sea of energy waves. The 4 percent of the waves which we have found inundates us with so much information, we sample only a billionth of what is available and simplify the information with concepts of time, color, weight, matter, and sight. Not only are perceptions of sight, sound, touch, and time misrepresented by our senses, we are also deceived into believing that we live throughout life as the same person. Our world is immaterial, and so are we. Somehow, we process bits of energy and create a video in our minds which portrays time, the motion of objects, and thoughts. Yet, "we" are dissolving and reforming trillions of times per second during this process, thus exchanging upixels with the universe. We are truly one with our world.

But what is life? What are we? In a quest to answer these questions, one can attempt an examination and understanding of the body, which started as one cell and grew to fifty trillion cells. How do all of those cells create a functional body, brain, and mind? If the future and all possible events exist, can we access some of them? How do we become conscious of just a portion of these events? And, if everything is space and energy, how can the body, brain, and mind be explained?

*My religion consists of a humble admiration of the illimitable superior spirit who reveals himself in the slight details we are able to perceive with our frail and feeble minds. That deeply emotional conviction of the presence of a superior reasoning power, which is revealed in the incomprehensible universe, forms my idea of God.*

–Albert Einstein

# WHAT ARE WE?

# 6
# BODY AND BRAIN

*Our environment and actions shape our brain's internal connec-*
*tions, the way we process information from the senses, and even*
*what aspects of the world we are able to perceive...For the rest*
*of our lives, however, our brains change constantly, reflecting*
*our life situations, the environment around us, the activities we*
*choose to pursue. Given the knowledge that we are what we do,*
*we can use our extraordinary human capacity for reason and*
*forethought to select how we want to program our own brains.*

–Robert Ornstein

Most people know that DNA is in every cell, and that it is the "blueprint" that codes for our bodies and brains. Even high school students can isolate and see their own DNA: Take ten drops of blood and ten drops of distilled water, then add a few drops of detergent. Add a couple of pinches of salt and filter the cloudy solution. Add forty drops of alcohol to the resultant clear liquid and place the mixture in a freezer. After ninety minutes, use a toothpick to pull out the web-like DNA.

How much DNA do I have? My fifty trillion cells would yield enough DNA to stretch to the moon and back 250,000 times. I began with six feet of DNA in one cell having nearly three billion bits of genetic information. This cell led to my body and brain. My body and brain create my reality, misperceptions and all. But how? What do scientists know about the body and brain?

The short answer to the second question is that scientists understand many of the mechanisms of the body and brain. However, I realized that this understanding has not been translated down to the quantum level. It is important to learn why and what is moving us toward a quantum perspective. I discovered the seemingly strange concepts of 21st-century science, which suggest that I must incorporate such thinking to resolve the question of how body and brain create mind/consciousness. Some scientists believe that only with a quantum perspective can we begin to answer the question of how the body and brain create reality, while other scientists disagree and believe quantum considerations are unnecessary. But first, let's see how our bodies were formed. How did the one cell with six feet of DNA become fifty trillion cells?

## HOW WERE WE FORMED?

The creation of the universe, the creation of life, and the evolutionary process are miracles of human existence. But so is the development of a human from a single fertilized egg. The formation of a baby reflects many aspects of evolution. As fetuses, we resemble other creatures, even having gill-like features.

My daughter, when she was young, asked me how old she was when she was born. Great question. All of our mothers had 250,000 follicles (which generate eggs) by their first menstruation, so half of all of our genes are older than our chronological age by decades. How were we formed then?

Each of us starts as a single cell, a fertilized egg, that combines the information contained in the genes of our mothers and fathers. About a hundred changes, called mutations, occur in the formation of this chimeric new being. Some of the genes are blended by cutting and splicing. Then, half of the genes are turned off. No matter how many times the two sources of information combine, no two fertilized eggs contain the same information. Nature shuffles the genetic deck and throws away half the cards.

At about day seven, this spherical collection of cells called an embryo implants itself into the mother's uterine lining. Of these cells, only a small number in the interior is destined to become the fetus. Many of those initial cells become the umbilical cord, placenta, and other structures. Around day thirteen, a groove-like structure develops down the middle of the mass of cells. This further organizes into three layers. The top layer becomes skin and nervous system, the next becomes muscle and bone, and the last becomes gut, pancreas, spleen, and liver. Teeth, appendages, and genitalia come from a combination of two of the layers.

At the end of week two, one has a head and a tail, front and a back, a right and a left. At about day 21, the brain begins to form. In the next four months, the brain adds about 500,000 neurons per minute. Vast numbers of neurons are destroyed in order for the brain to be wired properly. Cells between our fingers and toes die to provide the structure of those appendages. After four weeks, the fetus is less than half an inch long.

By day sixty, it is about an inch long and the forebrain, mid-brain, and hind brain are recognizable. The fetus begins kicking the mother at sixteen weeks. At week 34, the brain turns in the skull; the left hemisphere twists back and the right twists forward. By six months, sufficient central nervous system development occurs to receive, process, and store information. In the next several months before birth, the brain continues to produce about 250,000 neurons per minute.

We were born with all the neurons we will ever need—equal to that of an adult. So this is how we acquired the hardware to create our misperceptions. What about the adult body? What goes on there?

## BODY

For two centuries, scientists have been taking a reductionist, materialistic approach to understanding the body. Approaching the body as a machine and breaking down, or reducing, the parts to smaller components for better understanding have resulted in outstanding successes in medicine. At a cost of several billions of dollars, the genetic code of nearly three billion DNA units has been recorded, thus revealing possible solutions to illnesses. Applying this DNA knowledge to biotechnology will make hundreds of new drugs available for fighting diseases in the next decade.

The reductionists, however, stopped short of going down to the quantum level to understand the body. This is partly due to the materialistic perspective that most biologists and chemists have in thinking the world is made up of material, billiard ball-like entities rather than quantum stuff, or energy. It is also due to the fact that all of the body's cells are communicating in vast, complicated networks. These complex systems exhibit properties not reducible to their constituent parts.

Recently, a network perspective has led to a different approach to understanding the body. Emergence is a method of explaining complex organizational structures by using simple rules. Now, many scientists are focused on understanding networks. Each of our fifty trillion cells has thousands of chemical reactions that must be timed in correct sequence, for the correct duration, and finally turned off. Communications within and between the body's cells are orchestrated by hormones, peptides, steroids, immune cells, proteins, and a few hundred brain chemicals that connect to the complex network of brain cells, nerves, and spinal cord.

One network involving the immune system even leads our body to recognizing self from non-self. Almost all of our cells have identity tags that distinguish them from other humans' cells. This identity tag is encoded by DNA. If our immune system identifies an object not having this identity tag, it will mount an effort to rid the invader from us. This tag is unique to each of us. If we wish to receive tissue or an organ from another human, we must receive chemicals that prevent our immune systems from rejecting the foreign cells. In this sense, our immune systems quite literally define us.

Studies of complex networks have revealed how the body and brain communicate. They've also shown that one cannot truly understand one without some understanding of both. Some people might think, for example, that only the brain generates emotions. This is a false conclusion. Peptides, which are small proteins, have been shown to be important in emotions. These peptides exist not only in the brain but also throughout the body.

In the 1970s Candice Pert, a pharmacologist, discovered that brain cells have receptors that are like "locks" in the membranes of cells. These receptors interact with peptide "keys." Peptides seem to communicate between the body and brain. Perhaps most importantly, they also cause our emotions. These chemical peptides influence our moods, health, and are part of what defines us. When we have emotional thoughts, peptides are produced and spread throughout the body to influence us. These peptides may help explain the benefits of biofeedback, meditation, hypnosis, guided imagery, and prayer.

But the underlying purposes of our networks are to transform and utilize energy and to provide information.

ENERGY

We've made the case in earlier chapters that, at our core, we are a collection of upixels which are an unknown form of energy. So what is known about energy and the body?

The fact that we have energy flowing through us—a fact well accepted and utilized by the medical community—might be a significant clue to our existence and what we are. As discussed earlier, electrical energy is created by all living creatures. The energy produced by our tiny cellular bags pumping protons can be measured by modern machines. They define our states of health. In later chapters, I will describe other effects of the energy from these bags. Energy is a common metaphor, because science measures life's energy. Several Eastern traditions believe that life, and all else, is energy.

Energy can be utilized to perform work. Work takes place when moving muscles, while thinking, or in the functioning of our organs. We ingest food and drink, taking in calories that provide energy for our bodies. But we are more than a collection of bags of chemical reactions, which produce heat and burn calories. A closer examination illustrates that each of our cells creates electrical energy, and that energy is at the upixel or quantum realm.

Because of this cellular electrical energy, the body creates electromagnetic fields that can be recorded in electrocardiograms (ECGs) for heart condition diagnosis, and in electroencephalography (EEGs) for brain scans. An EEG is a recording of the electrical activity generated by the cerebral cortex, obtained from twenty or more electrodes placed on the scalp. The ECG is obtained with a voltage sensor designed to detect, amplify, and record the small voltage produced on the body's surface by cardiac electrical activity. The recordings give valuable information about the electrical output of the heart.

Our energy confers life. Abnormal ECG and EEG readings inform physicians of a patient's illness. When flat—no activity—they constitute a visual evidence of death. However, as we will discuss in a chapter on afterlife, even with flat responses, the consciousness and the mind might still exist! Energy abnormalities highlight opportunities for healing.

Robert Becker, a physician and proponent of the body's electrical properties, believed that understanding the energy aspects of our body will revolutionize medicine and science and lead to self-healing methods:

> I believe that these discoveries presage a revolution in biology and medicine…I believe this new knowledge will also turn medicine in the direction of greater humility, for we should see that whatever we achieve pales before the self-healing powers latent in all organisms.

A discussion of life's energy and self-healing will continue in later chapters.

The body's complex networks produce energy. These networks and the resulting energy are intimately linked to the brain. The brain transforms energy into information, but how?

## BRAIN

The network interactions of the brain are an important area of current research. Various complex networks within brain cells, among the cells of the brain, and from the brain to the rest of the body comprise the brain's total network. One result of this network is the production of energy and an electrical field. Understanding the brain requires an understanding of the "hard wiring," or cellular connections, genes, environment, and complex networks.

We have about 100 billion neurons. Neurons can fire up to 1,000 times per second. Each firing releases ions that eventually signal other neurons. Each neuron is connected to other neurons via 1,000-10,000 synapses. Synapses are tiny gaps in the connections between neurons, and it is the communication across these gaps that leads to neuronal activity.

Dean Hamer, a geneticist at the National Cancer Institute, made a conservative estimate that there are $10^{10,000,000,000}$—or one with ten billon zeros behind it—meaningful configurations (possible brain states that include memories and thoughts) in the brain. He sums up our brain power: "The take-home message is that our brains have more than enough computing power to handle every possible situation, to process every conceivable thought."

A node in a network is a point where many different connections are made. The brain's network develops and changes with time. Since neurons are connected to thousands of other neurons, they are the nodes of the brain. The brain suffers neurons dying all the time, increasingly with age. Therefore, numerous paths must exist to critical brain regions.

Even if large segments of the brain are removed or damaged, memories and functions can be retained via alternate pathways. Thus, having redundancy is an important aspect of a functional brain or any network.

The Internet is an example. The Internet is a complex network of millions of nodes—or computers—and requires redundancy when connections are broken. A significant portion of the Internet's connections could be damaged or destroyed, yet the Internet remains functional. An important transatlantic fiber-optical cable that carries trillions of bits of information per second could be damaged, yet the Internet would reroute the messages and continue to function.

## BRAIN VERSUS SUPERCOMPUTERS: NOTHING MATCHES THE BRAIN

Is the human brain the ultimate portable computer? The human brain is not like a computer or even a cluster of supercomputers. The three-pound brain uses less energy than a light bulb and stores the equivalent of ten million thousand-page books while helping to control all of our fifty trillion cells' biochemical and electrical activities. Even a thousand supercomputers could not perform the simple cognitive and creative functions that one brain does, let alone produce consciousness.

In a computer, millions of transistors interact. However, no transistor has the capacity to control which other transistors it strengthens its connections to. This is but one of the features our neurons have for creating long-term memories. The firings of particular neurons strengthen particular connections to other neurons. Additionally, the brain has hundreds of chemicals for communication that have no analogy with current computers. Compared to computers, our brains are vastly more complex in design and operation.

We can learn, be self-aware, distinguish patterns, shapes, and shades, and interpret what an image, such as a figure or a face in abstract art, might represent. We can create a story from a picture and utilize a sensation, such as a taste or smell, to recall a memory. We can quickly access memories to help guide our actions. Most computers cannot perform these functions. Thus, although there are some similarities between the human brain and the workings of a computer, computers cannot truly give insight into how our upixels create thought or mind.

A better source of comparison to the human brain is the brain of an ancestor. What clues about our brains do we have from our early ancestors? Evolution supplies some of the answers.

## THE BRAIN'S ELEMENTS AND ITS UNIQUENESS

Our brains retain elements of the early reptilian brain and the early mammalian brain. The brain of a reptile is focused solely on survival. This included digestion, circulation, respiration, and reproduction. The brains of the early mammals were more sophisticated, with a limbic system (or mid-brain) which yielded the capacity for emotion, coordination of movement, and the fight-or-flight response. With these higher brain functions, the early mammals were responsible for the demise of many species of reptiles.

Humans and primates added a third component to the brain—the cerebral cortex, an approximately one-eighth-inch-thick layer of wrinkled matter on the top and front. The cortex allows us to have abilities in language, mathematics, and problem-solving. The cortex also aids in the development of memory and creativity.

Not all brains are the same. Nutrition before and after birth, drugs, alcohol, and genetics all play a role in the brain's health. Einstein's brain was found to be interestingly different, missing a fold, thus allowing better and faster communication between neurons.

Some individuals have brains whose signals are amplified. Robert Ornstein, a psychologist and author of numerous books on the brain, calls them "high-gain people." These people seek quiet and solitude. So-called low-gain people are the opposite and seek outside stimulation.

The diversity of human brains suggests that, as with fingerprints, individuals have their own unique hardware. But how does all the diverse hardware acquire the ability to learn, think, move, perceive, speak, imagine, remember, create a unique personality?

## BRAIN GROWTH AND DEVELOPMENT

We are born with only about 25 percent of the size and weight of our adult brains. As explained earlier, a newborn infant has nearly all of the neurons of an adult. If this is the case, then why does it need to add size and weight.

The brain of a baby is more like an unassembled brain than one ready for the world. Neurons die and reassemble during and following birth. The weight and size gain of the brain is due to the expansion of the neurons, the branching of the brain cells, other modifications of the neurons, the addition of billions of glia cells, and the generation of new blood vessels to supply the growing brain with nutrients. Numerous reasons exist for this lengthy process of assembling and developing the brain. One of many has to do with the eyes and visual system. Ornstein summarizes the situation:

> ...visual systems that need to adapt to changing head size during development have to undergo constant reevaluation and change so that stability is maintained from the time of birth to time of maturity. Fixing the visual system at one specification would never work.

In addition to these cellular changes (i.e. new blood vessels and glia cells) in the growing child's brain, the brain is also developing by strengthening connections. All of these represent a partial explanation of the importance of timing in learning and in the development of the personality.

The following table is a highly abbreviated summary of this fascinating process.

Table 4. Age and the Assembly of the Human Brain

| Age | Event | Comments |
|---|---|---|
| Nine to five months before birth | Beginning about three weeks after conception, brain forms and rapidly adds neurons. | About 500,000 neurons per minute are being added. By 60 days after conception, the forebrain, midbrain, and hind brain can be recognized. |
| Five months before birth to birth | A slight decrease in the rate of addition of new neurons. | Rate of new neurons might be about 250,000 per minute. |
| Birth | Baby has 100 billion neurons or more, and many times as many glia cells. | Spinal cord and brain stem are fully organized. Brain weighs about 400 grams and has about as many neurons as the adult will have. Brain stem and spinal cord help control bodily functions. |
| 0-3 months | Modification of the cells of the cerebellum and mid-brain. | Glia cells are being added, neurons are branching and expanding; new blood vessels are added. |

| Three months to 1 year | Modifications to the forebrain and cerebral cortex begin at about the end of first year. | Motor coordination and sensory processing are first addressed. |
|---|---|---|
| 1-20 years | Forebrain and cerebral cortex regions are sequentially developed. | Perception, memory, judgment and language, followed in later years by planning abilities, intentionality, and further refinements to personality. |

By the age of five the brain has reached 90 percent of its size. A chimpanzee takes only about 22 months to reach this stage, but the more complex human brain requires a longer time to create the proper wiring. With such capabilities, it can perceive our world, attempt to understand our existence, contemplate our purpose, and become spiritual. This means a parent must protect a child for several years while the child's brain is developing. In the early history of humans, evolution thus favored the survival of protected children over neglected ones.

## AGE VERSUS CRITICAL ACTIVITIES IN CHILDREN

Human babies hear in the womb and recognize songs after birth. Babies also seem to distinguish pitch and rhythm, leading one to believe that babies come pre-wired for music. Robert Zatorre, a neuroscientist at the Montreal Neurological Institute, remarked:

> …babies are surprisingly sophisticated mini-musicians: they are able to distinguish different scales and chords, and show preferences for consonant over dissonant combinations…

They can recognize tunes played to them over periods of days
or weeks.

Later in their development, faces, gestures, and the voices of care-
givers are recognized. At about age eight months, the baby becomes
quite upset when the mother is absent.

The fact that the human brain is prepared to adapt to its world to a
large extent is illustrated with a summary of child development.

Table 5. Age and Critical Activities

| Age months/ years | Activity | Comments |
|---|---|---|
| 0-1 month | Random and reflex actions. | Reflexively sucks objects. |
| 1-4 months | Discriminates shapes and forms. | If object disappears, baby believes it no longer exists. |
| 4-8 months | Imitates more complex actions, does not reach for objects. | If object is placed into hand, baby will grasp it. All 869 sounds or phonemes can be recognized. This ability is slowly lost after this age. |
| 8-12 months | Reaches for objects; enjoys "Peek-a-Boo" (face appearing and disappearing behind hands). | Anticipates the reappearance of the face. |

| 12-18 months | Explores toys of different shapes and sizes, intentionally drops and observes the dropping object. | Learns new ways of doing same act. |
|---|---|---|
| 18-24 months | Begins to think before acting. | Attempts to anticipate reactions. |
| 2-4 years | Uses language and mental images, attempts to generalize in illogical ways, and believes that inanimate objects are alive. | At age three a vocabulary of about 1,000 words (limit of a chimpanzee is about 150 words). Believes natural phenomena are manmade. |
| 4-5 years | Beginning to understand logical sequences of objects. | At age four a vocabulary of about 4,000 words. Languages learned after age six will have an accent. |

This summary covers but a small fraction of the key learning events that a child experiences. The development of the brain continues into the teen years.

The wiring of the brain results in what we are and who we become. However, our attempts to understand reality and all of our perceptions and misperceptions come from information received from outside the brain. This brings us to our connections to the outside world.

## OUR SENSES: THE SOURCE OF OUR MISPERCEPTIONS AND OUR REALITY

We've made the case that what is really out there is space and energy.

Only about 4 percent of our world is the form of energy we can detect and, of that, only a billionth is recognized by our senses. In the last chapter we explored how our sight is the result of information gathered by visible light in relation to interaction with various forms of energy. Our brains compile this information and paint a mental image of our world.

The eyes' complex interaction with the brain is an active area of research. Scientists know more about sight than hearing. Only recently have they documented the network of reactions set in motion by sound waves vibrating along the hair cells of the inner ear.

Consider the Emperor Penguin, whose newly-hatched chick initially has only the father to care for it, the mother having left to feed herself. The father later leaves to seek food for himself and the baby. Upon his return, the chick must recognize the unique call of his father, and the father in turn must recognize the unique call of the chick. This often occurs in high winds and against a background din of thousands of other fathers and chicks calling for each other. The failure of keen sound recognition could result in the death of the infant.

Although many animals have more sensitive hearing, our brains process sounds to interpret rhythm, pitch, and melody, and to experience evoked emotion, such as remembrances of a lost love, a happy or sad occurrence, or even nationalism. We can also tune out sounds. When we concentrate, even in a noisy room, the sound seems to diminish markedly or disappear.

The importance of smells and tastes, and their roles in our perceptions and memories, is best illustrated with an example. Ornstein uses the example of a person who attended an opera and then dined on his favorite food, steak with béarnaise sauce. He became ill that night. From that night on, he felt an aversion to his favorite sauce. He did not develop an aversion to the opera, steak, his wife, with whom he had dinner, or his friend, from whom he caught the flu. He associated the smell and taste of the sauce more closely to the negative experience than any object or person.

Tastes and smells are created by molecules (agglomerates of upixels). Sensors on our tongues and in our nasal cavities detect and transmit the molecules' information to the brain. The brain creates the sensation as well as triggers any emotional response. Taste and smell lead to conclusions by our brain as to what is attractive to eat and what is not. It is information that sound and sight cannot deliver.

## SENSES ENABLE US TO SURVIVE, NOT EXPERIENCE TRUE REALITY

Our five senses—sight, sound, touch, taste, and smell—provide a minuscule sampling of the environment and the larger universe. The human body and brain have evolved sufficiently to allow us to sense a small portion of the light spectrum, hear a fraction of the sound waves moving through air, smell and taste a few hundred molecules, and sense by touch a small fraction of the molecules, vibrations, and waves that interact with us.

We possess only about a third of the number of functioning olfactory genes as mice. We cannot see as extensive a spectrum of light as a tiger can. Why did we develop such limitations?

Perhaps the human cerebral cortex has resulted in so much activity that the more subtle senses are not needed. Even our advanced brains, the most evolved in the known universe, cannot handle all the information and sensations of the world "out there." Our brains are filters. Nearly all that is out there is not realized or recognized by the brain. The brain concentrates its efforts on analyzing the information from a hundredth of a billionth of what is out there. As discussed earlier, our senses do not—and cannot—give us a true picture of reality.

My body and brain are responsible for my views of reality, as well as my perceptions and misperceptions. What about the role played by my mind? Can the mind be fully explained by the brain? If the world is mental, and if I melt by exchanging molecules and upixels with the universe at each instant, then how are mind and consciousness generated? And is mind "out there" or inside my head?

This brings me to two topics that have been debated for centuries by philosophers, religious believers, and scientists—consciousness and the so-called mind-matter problem. If there is to be a true healing of the rift between science and spirituality, these topics need to be reconciled.

> *The cell is a machine driven by energy. It can thus be approached*
> *by studying matter, or by studying energy.*
>
> –Albert Szent-Gyorgyi

# 7

# THE MIND-MATTER PROBLEM AND CONSCIOUSNESS

*All that we are is the result of what we have thought. The mind is everything. What we think, we become.*

–Maharishi Mahesh Yogi

I am a couch potato engaged in the great American pastime—flipping through TV channels. I am too cheap to subscribe to *TV Guide,* so instead, I pay the price by looking for the needle in the haystack. Translation: I attempt to find the one TV channel out of hundreds that might be of interest to me. One day, I come across a channel with a Road Runner cartoon.

I remember, decades ago, watching Wile E. Coyote being stymied by the Road Runner. Before I realize it, I watch the entire brightly colored cartoon with the "beep-beeps" blasting through my surround-sound speakers and Wile E. Coyote falling into canyons and smashing into walls while the Road Runner zips along at blurring speed across my TV screen.

I feel guilty about my regression to childhood and return to writing this book. Then it hits me. My being immersed in this cartoon is exactly what I needed to exemplify materialism. During the time that I was watching it, I did not question the reality of seeing animated animals perform outlandish feats. My mind simply accepted the happenings. Only afterwards did I fully realize the fantasy world I entered.

My perceiving the world is similar to watching the cartoon. I perceive the world as being made up of material stuff such as buildings, earth, and people. I do not question colors, sights, sounds, or tastes.

Yet the world out there is different. My mind creates all of these images and sensations so that I can make sense of this place in which I live. Thus, my perceptions of the world do not match the logic of what are really out there—energy, space, dark matter, dark energy, and information. I accept the current scientific theories that my world is quite different and that the "material stuff" is made up of quantum entities and energy. But the quantum world is not what I perceive. Therefore, in a very real sense, I myself am living in a cartoon world and perceiving only caricatures of reality. We all are.

What creates this cartoon world? Of course, most of us would point to our brains. What is mind then?

My definition of mind is the ability to perceive surroundings and have emotions, imagination, memory, and will, as well as process information consciously and unconsciously.

## MIND AND THE MIND-MATTER PROBLEM

Many scientists take a traditional materialistic perspective on the mind, believing that it can be explained completely by the actions of the brain. When pressed, they will concede that the body is also involved.

The mind-matter problem, also known as the mind-body problem, poses the question: how do we explain the mind using matter? Most people accept that, without matter, i.e. the brain and the body, the mind would not exist. Most scientists would agree that when all brain activities cease, the mind is gone, although a later discussion of near-death experiences challenges this belief.

Are the upixels important in understanding the mind, or just irrelevant detail? A materialist would say our inner universes of mind and consciousness are solely due to the cellular and molecular components of our brains, the neurons, the spaces between them (the synapses), the glia cells, and the hundreds of chemical communicators. The materialist regards his theories as sufficient to explain the mind without quantum considerations.

This reductionist, materialist perspective would therefore equate the brain's activities with consciousness and mind. Looking at the quantum level would be like attempting to find meaning in this sentence by taking a powerful electron microscope and examining each and every speck of ink and each fiber of the paper at the atomic level. Such scrutiny is exactly what must be done according to quantum-brain advocates. Why?

The materialistic perspective is an 18th-century perspective. I have presented the 21st-century perspective of reality focused, not on materials, but on energy and upixels.

We now know that to decipher the book of reality, we must look beyond the sentences of molecules, the words of atoms, the letters of elementary particles, and even the microscopic ink specks of upixels. Understanding comes from all of these components, the blank space of the vacuum, and, finally, the source of the information. Without finding the rules that will decipher this invisible message into something that we can understand, we are missing the information of the message. This is the rationale that scientists use to examine the quantum level for processes that might reveal clues to mind and consciousness.

Materialism is the belief that only the physical is real. If mind and consciousness are merely a physical, mechanical result of brain activities, then it is logical that, after death, nothing survives. This is the belief of many in the West, but it conflicts with most spiritual and religious teachings. Materialism, therefore, is responsible for part of the rift that exists between science and spirituality. Can science bridge the rift by showing us another view of mind and matter? What about the quantum-brain perspective?

It is important to note that scientists do not doubt that at the smallest level of what we call matter are quantum entities undergoing quantum processes. What has not been proved is whether understanding the quantum level will lead to a better understanding of mind and consciousness. The payoff could be reconciling science and spirituality.

## MIND-MATTER THEORIES

Can neurons, the brain, and the body fully explain the mind? There are numerous theories. The following table outlines six of them.

Table 6. Mind-Matter Theories

| Theory | Description | Comments |
|---|---|---|
| Functional-ism | Mind s a brain state. The theory denies the existence of consciousness. | There is no mind-matter problem—all is matter. |
| Epiphenom-enalism | Mind is real but cannot affect the physical world. Brain is the cause of all aspects of mind. Mind doesn't cause anything to happen (the brain already did it). | Consciousness cannot act on the physical world—example: moving a finger. |
| Emergent Materialism | Mind arises from brain by only brain's activities, but cannot be predicted by brain proccesses. Mind can affect mental and physical change. | Mental activities can affect neurons. No need to involve quantum explanations. |
| "Agnostic" Physicalism | Mind is a result of brain. There may be non-material forces. The brain must change before the mind changes. | "Agnostic" refers to the possible existence of non-material forces, not the rejection of religion. |

| Process Philosophy | Mind and brain are manifestations of the same reality, but in a constant flux–both are processes. | Consistent with quantum theory. |
|---|---|---|
| Dualistic Interactioism | Mind and conscious-ness can be indepen-dent of brain. May be non-materialistic basis for mind. | Some of those who suscribe to this theory believe in life after death. |

Functionalism denies the existence of a mind-matter problem be-cause everything is matter. The mind is simply the result of brain pro-cesses. Epiphenomenalism and emergent materialism are similar and essentially state that mind arises only from brain activities. Agnostic physicalism teaches that mind is a result of brain, but adherents hedge their bets by stating that there might be non-material forces. Such forces, however, must first influence brain states. The dualistic interac-tionism school teaches that mind and consciousness can be indepen-dent of the brain and the mind can shape the brain. Basically, five of these theories either argue that all can be explained by the brain or that the mind might have a non-material basis.

Process philosophy holds that mind and brain are realized by a single reality, but one that is in constant flux. Process philosophy was greatly influenced by Alfred North Whitehead, mathematician and philosopher. His 1929 book, *Process and Reality*, laid the foundation for this theory. Whitehead believed that the worldview changed in the last four centuries from space and matter to process, due to the insights gained in the 20th century that matter is a form of energy and energy is sheer activity. Hence, process.

Jeffrey Schwartz and Sharon Begley in their book, *The Mind and the Brain*, comment on process philosophy:

It thus is compatible with classical Buddhist philosophy, which views clear and penetrating awareness of change imperma- nence...Thus, as Whitehead put it, 'The reality is the process,' and it is a process made up of vital transient 'drops of experi- ence, complex and interdependent.'This view is strikingly con- sistent with recent developments in quantum physics.

People often use the term "consciousness." Could we have mind without consciousness? Is consciousness part of the mind? We have numerous definitions of consciousness. Some are circular, such as the state of being conscious. I define consciousness as the state we are in when we are aware of our surroundings or thoughts and aware that we are aware of them.

## CONSCIOUSNESS

As with the mind-matter problem, we have numerous views of con- sciousness. Here are some of the diverse explanations of consciousness

Table 7.  Consciousness Beliefs

| Belief | Comments |
|---|---|
| Dualism: An essence given to humans from a God or other out- side source | Believes that physical sci- ence cannot understand consciousness |
| Idealist monism: A mental state | The universe is entirely a construct of the mind or spiritual |

| | |
|---|---|
| Material monism: Totally physical explanation | The only reality is material or physical. Some believe it arises from only one or a few sources in the brain. Others believe that consciousness comes from a collective involving many regions and parts of the brain |
| Quantum processes | Quantum processes are involved in consciousness |
| A philisophical matter | Not a matter for science |

In reviewing the various theories on mind-matter and consciousness, I have found that most fall into one of two catagories:

1. Mind/consciousness/God is our reality.

2. Matter is the basis for mind and consciousness.

### A VOICE FROM THE PAST

My research led me to an individual, who had interesting insights and believed that reality is spiritual, an idealist monist belief. He believed that other universes exist, space is not empty, the fundamental elements of the universe are forces and not matter, and all is a plenum— that is, all elements are interconnected, as suggested by the principle of nonlocality we discussed in Chapter 4. Although these concepts are consistent with 21st-century science, Gottfried Wilhelm Leibniz wrote these concepts three centuries ago.

Leibniz is credited as the co-inventor of calculus along with Isaac Newton. He constructed the first mechanical calculator and developed the modern form of the binary numeral system used in digital computers. In the 17th and 18th centuries, when Leibniz lived, the "philosophies" encompassed science, religion, and philosophy. Natural philosophy was science, religious philosophy was theology, and practical philosophy was ethics.

Leibniz's publication became known as the *Monadology*. Much of the teachings of the 90 sections utilized his knowledge of science, calculus, and advanced mathematics, and his unique logic. He was aware of Chinese philosophy, which in turn was influenced by Mahayana Buddhism, and both had concepts similar to his. Many of his insights thus go back 2,000 years. In the *Monadology*, *Theodicy*, and related papers, Leibniz described the most basic units of the universe, monads, and their relationship to all matter, creatures, and God. He was the first great philosopher or scientist to combine:

1. The insight that the basic units of change in the world, monads, are immaterial and too subtle to be perceived.

2. The principle that change is physical, resulting in some of the inherently active functions of the mind.

In keeping with Leibniz's first point, quantum processes, too, are immaterial and cannot be perceived, resulting in the wave/particle dilemma. His second point is consistent with process philosophy which maintains that flux or change of a single reality results in mind. This is also consistent with quantum processes appearing as matter and mind.

## SO WHICH THEORY IS CORRECT?

In philosophy, definitions and precise articulation of thoughts are essential. Author and philosopher Matthew Stewart reveals that Leibniz pointed out the semantics problem three centuries ago: "Leibniz, like a number of more recent philosophers, cherished the notion that there are no genuine philosophical conflicts; there is only bad grammar. "

Or are there genuine philosophical conflicts caused by semantics?

## REALMS OF REALITY

In examining semantics, "matter" is composed of upixels, and it can be regarded as either material or immaterial, depending on one's perspective. A definition of matter is a substance that occupies space and has weight. Matter as defined by physicists is a form of energy subject to the influence of gravity and thus has weight as discussed in Chapter 5. But energy is immaterial. So, is the philosophical debate, at least in part, a result of our concept of matter?

You'll recall that in Chapter 4, observation (or consciousness) caused the upixel to change from a wave to a particle. Mind and consciousness result in quantum processes becoming "particle-like" since observation converts the probability wave of the upixels into particles. All processes involving energy or molecules such as neurons involve quantum processes. At the core of matter are the upixels involved in quantum processes.

Figure 1. Realms of Reality

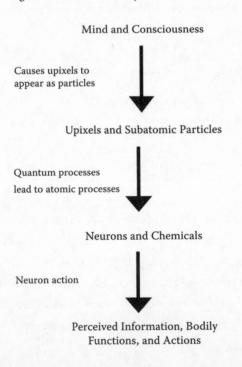

Mind and Consciousness

Causes upixels to
appear as particles

Upixels and Subatomic Particles

Quantum processes
lead to atomic processes

Neurons and Chemicals

Neuron action

Perceived Information, Bodily
Functions, and Actions

Note the consistency of this explanation of mind to the explanation of the realms of reality in our universe, as discussed in Chapter 4, Table 3. There we covered the various realms of reality—information, space or the vacuum, quantum, and atomic. Mind and consciousness emerge from the information realm, upixels and subatomic particles from the quantum realm, and neurons and chemicals from the realm we notice—the atomic—our perceived reality. This explanation is consistent with, or has elements in common with, the idealist monist, process philosophy, Leibniz's monads, and quantum processes presented earlier.

Not apparent in Figure 1 is the collective unconscious—that part of everyone's unconscious that is instincts, forms, or symbols. Indeed, many philosophers and psychologists deny the existence of Jung's collective unconscious. Perhaps the archetypal wisdom of the collective unconscious comes from either the upixels or the information realm. We'll cover more on this in the next chapter.

Thus, the answer to the mind-matter question as to whether matter creates mind is NO. But consciousness, mind, upixels, and matter are nested aspects of reality, just as information, vacuum, quantum, and atomic realms are all part of our reality.

Figure 1 posits that mind or consciousness changes the brain, since mind can affect upixels, and upixels affect neurons. Neurons and the brain allow information of the world at large to emerge. But it was mind that began the process. Mind changes brain. Is there any evidence for this?

The dogma held by most scientists until the 1990s was that the brain cannot be significantly changed after adolescence. As the quotation by Ornstein at the beginning of Chapter 6 indicates, this belief has changed. Furthermore, due to modern technology that enables imaging of the brain with machines, our ability to change the brain is a proven fact.

## CHANGING YOUR MIND

Jeffrey Schwartz, a neuroscientist at UCLA, found that the mind can reshape or rewire the adult brain. Schwartz, in his decades of work with obsessive-compulsive disorder (OCD), found that patients following his therapy produced changes in their neural pathways. This work is highly significant. It proves that the mind can cause healing.

Obsessive-compulsive disorder often yields devastating consequences. The unwanted urges to incessantly wash one's hands or to constantly worry if a door was left unlocked can prevent individuals from holding a job or retaining relationships. We discussed in Chapter 6 how, unlike computers, the brain can reinforce neural connections. Schwartz had his patients focus their attention on alternative thoughts, such as going out to the garden, rather than washing their hands. This strengthened the neural connections that result in the thought of going to the garden and weakened the OCD urge connections. Brain scans showed that as the patients improved, their brain wiring changed.

Richard Restak, a neurologist and neuropsychiatrist, reminds us that our brains change every day due to our environment and thoughts:

> We now recognize that our brain isn't limited by considerations that are applicable to machines. Thoughts, feelings, and actions, rather than mechanical laws, determine the health of our brain.

The discovery that we can change our brains, called brain plasticity, has several important implications:

1. The mind and brain are not machinelike.

2. The mind and brain are not solely governed by genes and inheritance.

3. We have free will, meaning that we are sometimes in a position to impact the future.

4. The environment influences the mind and brain; therefore, who we are is, in part, determined by our world.

## PLASTIC BRAINS AND QUANTUM THEORY

Schwartz and his collaborator, Henry Pierce Stapp, a quantum physicist, believe that neuroplasticity, the ability to shape neuron connections, can be explained using quantum mechanics. Quantum theory
allows intention and attention to affect real physical effects on the
brain, but how?

In the preceding OCD example, potential brain connections trigger the thought of going to the garden while other connections trigger
the thought of washing one's hands. Schwartz and Stapp point out
that in the neuron is a vesicle that has the potential to release ions.
They note that this vesicle exists as "a superposition of quantum wave
functions, one representing 'release' and one representing 'don't release.'
This is true in the brain circuit for washing as well as for gardening."

### QUANTUM THEORY ALLOWS THESE STATES TO COEXIST

The OCD patient originally had a higher probability in releasing
the ions from the vesicles governing the circuit for washing hands.
Schwartz and Stapp contend that, with the attention and mental effort, the patient is able by virtue of quantum processes to change the
odds, increasing the probability of releasing the ions from the vesicles
governing the gardening circuit. The gardening circuit is strengthened.
With time and repeated attention, the gardening circuit's vesicles increase their probability of firing.

Schwartz and Stapp use a quantum rationale to explain the changes in the brains of OCD patients, but are they the only scientists who
believe that quantum processes are critical to the mind and brain? No.
Many scientists in the 21st century are suggesting that quantum processes help explain the actions of the brain. But what are the "vesicles"
that Schwartz and Stapp invoke to explain a quantum-mind connection?

## THE QUANTUM BRAIN/MIND

The number of advocates of the quantum-mind theory has grown rapidly in the last decade. Quantum-brain/mind theories are quite complex. But at the heart of the theory must be a rationale as to how a quantum event relates, albeit via numerous and complex steps, to mind and consciousness. Both the materialists and the quantum-mind advocates need to provide an explanation for the processes resulting in mind and consciousness. I find no explanation from the materialists. However, quantum advocates provide such a theory. Jeffery Satinover, author of *The Quantum Brain*, coined the term "smart wires" as a metaphor to help explain the theory of how neurons utilize quantum processes. Since brain science is complex and involves numerous terms and jargon, we'll explore the concept with a metaphor.

## SMART WIRING—A METAPHOR FOR THE BRAIN'S QUANTUM PROCESSES

In all living organisms, including bacteria, a microscopic set of smart wires provides intelligence and computational capabilities. These wires are hollow and the "hole" is the size of a few atoms. Quantum entities such as protons and electrons pass through the hole, resulting in chemical bond changes and alterations in the wire's shape.

In bacteria, the shape change drives appendages, allowing movement toward food or away from undesirable environments, a clear indication of the ability to sense and respond to surroundings. In human brains, such wire shape changes lead to a neuron firing, resulting in thought, memory, and mind. Thus, the quantum happenings of this wire help define life by endowing intelligence.

Now that we've viewed the concept of these smart wires, I will explain some of the details of the actual theory. Chemists call these smart wires "microtubules."

## MICROTUBULES, QUANTUM PROCESSES, AND MIND

Some scientists believe that microtubules present in neurons are where quantum processes lead to mind. Within a network of billions of neurons, each connected to thousands of synapses, is an inner network of trillions of microtubules. Microtubules are made up of several proteins that form a microscopic hollow cylinder. The cylinders are linked in a network resembling microscopic wires, hence the term "smart wire." Biochemical reactions within microtubules set off a vibratory wave, resulting in shape changes in the wire. These, in turn, cause neuron firing. The resulting neuronal change then signals other microtubule networks in other neurons to effect further changes in the brain.

Microtubules, or similar structures, are found in all life, even in simple one-celled organisms such as amoebas or paramecia.

So microtubules explain the action of neurons. But can one go down to the upixel level to explain the brain processes and mind? This would be the quantum connection.

Quantum entities have probabilities of several configurations, locations, and states. This unpredictability is called the uncertainty principle. This uncertainty of quantum events, such as the position of an electron, was discussed in Chapters 4 and 5. Let's take a voyage into the brain cells of the OCD patient Schwartz and Stapp discussed earlier. Within this brain are neurons that, if fired, will lead to the OCD urge. Other neurons, if fired, would result in the patient going into the garden instead. As with pistol triggers ready to be pulled, within all of those neurons are microtubules that possess quantum states prepared to go either way—fire or not fire. What decides which trigger is pulled? Quantum events in the hollow portion of the microtubules—electrons and protons moving through the hole—create shape changes.

Some quantum-brain advocates believe that the focused intention of going into the garden triggers quantum events within the hollow portion of a microtubule, resulting in its shape change. This results in the activation of the neuron that initiates the action of the patient spending time in the garden. This change within the neuron would be instantly communicated to all of the other neurons through nonlocality, since the upixel causing the action is entangled with other upixels in the brain, and the brain state would then change.

THE QUANTUM MIND

Other variations of this quantum-mind theory also exist, but more evidence is needed to convince many scientists to embrace it. Numerous renowned scientists do, however, subscribe to a quantum basis for the mind. One of them is Freeman Dyson, a great 20th-century physicist, mathematician, and Princeton University professor, who said:

> It appears that mind, as manifested by the capacity to make choices [free will], is to some extent inherent in every electron...it is reasonable to believe in the existence of...a mental component of the universe. If we believe in this mental component of the universe, then we can say that we are small pieces of God's mental apparatus.

Perhaps the logic of all of these quests for quantum explanations of mind and consciousness might be summarized in a quotation from Nobel Prize-winning physicist Eugene Wigner:

> The laws of quantum mechanics cannot be formulated...without recourse to the concept of consciousness...It seems inconsistent to explain the state of the mind of [an] observer...in terms of concepts, such as positions of atoms, which have to be explained, then, in terms of the content of consciousness...The extreme materialistic point of view...is clearly absurd and...is also in conflict with the tenets of quantum mechanics.

## MATERIALISM—AN OUTDATED METAPHOR

The rift between science and spirituality closes when, instead of holding on to the dogma of 19th-century materialism, we employ the teachings of 20th- and 21st-century sciences: that the basic units of the universe are upixels that are some form of energy. Energy is immaterial, yet it can be converted to what humans call matter when the upixels agglomerate to form more complex entities. We learned that what are really out there are mind, consciousness, and information. Astrophysicist Arthur Eddington cautioned us that science often tells us more about ourselves than about the external universe:

> We have found a strange footprint on the shores of the unknown. We have devised profound theories, one after another, to account for its origin. At last, we have succeeded in reconstructing the creature that made the footprint. And lo! It is our own.

The Western paradigm is that brain creates mind and consciousness, yet it cannot offer an explanation or evidence in support of this assertion. It is as though we were to watch a movie on television and insist that it was created by the TV. I have presented an explanation and evidence that mind and consciousness emerge from brain activities. But mind and consciousness are derived from the information realm, and it is upixels, operating via quantum processes, that effect neuronal changes and result in the emergence of information. We'll discuss further evidence to support this model in later chapters.

Our cartoon world of caricatures that we call matter is wedged between the seemingly strange world of the very small, containing the upixels and the energy of the vacuum, and the incredibly large universe that houses parallel universes, dark energy, and dark matter—and all of these exist on the stage of the fleeting drama we call life. Free will allows us to choose which moments to include in our story from all the possibilities that exist in the infinite universe.

## WHAT IS LIFE? AND, WHAT ARE WE?

Our existence in the greater scheme of things might seem insignificant, like a grain of sand on one of an infinite number of beaches. As scientists now know, we can change our brains and, through such change, we can heal our minds. The basis for such healing might also heal the rift between science and spirituality, since we are just beginning to realize the mind's full potential. The universe is mind and consciousness. The potential seems limitless.

Evidence that our minds can reshape our brains is strong evidence of free will. With free will and self-determination, humans have the power to control at least part of their future. Perhaps, when acting in unison with common vision and purpose, human minds can shape the course of our world, the quintessential example of free will.

We now know that the mind can change the brain. The mind has been known for some time to heal psychological states and the body. Let me move to examples of the mind performing healings, exploring even a mind-gene connection.

> *Mind no longer appears as an accidental intruder into the realm*
> *of matter; we are beginning to suspect that we ought rather to*
> *hail it as the creator and governor of the realm of matter.*

> –Sir James Hopwood Jeans

# 8

# THE HEALING MIND

*The brain converts the neural messages of mind into "messenger molecules" of the body. These...can direct the endocrine system to produce steroid hormones that can reach into the nucleus of different cells of the body to produce the various molecules that will regulate metabolism...in sickness and health. There really is a mind-gene connection! Mind ultimately does modulate the creation and expression of the molecules of life!*

—Ernest Lawrence Rossi

I was fortunate enough to grow up in a poor family. Before I was born, my parents lived for a while in an abandoned boxcar—the two of them, that is, plus three children. My siblings and I worked to make it through grade school. The summer months in the Central Valley of California often reached temperatures of 105 degrees Fahrenheit or higher but we all helped our parents in the agricultural fields as farm laborers.

One of my earliest jobs was spreading grapes out on wood or paper trays, where they would dry and turn into raisins. The wood trays were heavy, and the hot nails in them burned my hands, but the lighter paper trays sometimes cut my fingers as I spread them out. At the corners of the paper trays I set clods of dirt to keep the hot wind from blowing them away. In the afternoon, after a dried-out sandwich and a warm soda under a dusty vine, I could not keep up.

My father would lay out his own trays. As he dumped the grapes from a pan onto the trays, and I would spread them out and remove the leaves. Around us the rows of vines were about a quarter of a mile long. As I tried to see the end of the row, the summer heat would cause the distant grape vines to shimmer.

In those days, every penny counted. My father earned about five cents per tray. A good day produced 300 to 400 trays, or about $15-$20.

Except for this memory, I don't remember much of my childhood. When I studied hypnosis, the instructor guided me into a trance and I regressed to my early years. Only a single image emerged: an endless row of grapes, dumped on trays and ready to be spread. The image occurred in the late afternoon, after we'd started the workday at about 5:30 in the morning. I was five or six years old. The dirt on my face mixed with my tears and fell onto the trays.

This was my first experience of regression analysis, the technique used to recall a past event hidden from normal memory. With the correct techniques, regression therapy can heal the problems caused by the suppressed memory. The poverty of my early childhood had made me ashamed of my past, and I had buried my more painful memories.

When people asked what my parents did for a living, I answered with a half-truth. "Farming," I'd say. However, this session indelibly reframed my mind. To me, my poverty became a gift, and I was never to be ashamed of my childhood or my parents ever again. My parents gave me the gift of growing up poor. Poverty taught me and my siblings that we could either get a good education or become farm laborers. We all chose to work our way through college.

The hypnotic-regression session described above occurred in the 1980s, when I first began learning hypnosis. I was interested in how the mind facilitates healing. Hypnosis is one of numerous methods that enable the mind to heal.

The quotation at the beginning of this chapter is by Ernest Rossi, a clinical psychologist and the author of many books on hypnosis. Hypnosis is defined as producing an altered state of consciousness that can also be characterized as a trancelike state, which detaches the subject from his physical surroundings as in contemplation or daydreaming. These states can cause the nucleus of cells to produce chemicals. This is done through the action of activating DNA in the nucleus to begin the network of reactions, which results in the production of the desired chemical. Indeed, mind causes changes at the DNA level.

## HYPNOSIS

The father of modern hypnotherapy was Milton Erickson, a medical doctor, clinical psychologist, and clinical psychiatrist. One of his patients, a woman in her 30s, had an irregular menstrual cycle. Erickson noted that, "Her periods resulted in severe headaches, vomiting, gastrointestinal disturbances, and actual invalidism for five days." She wanted help without psychotherapy, but she consented to hypnosis at Erickson's direction.

During the trance, Erickson suggested that she choose one night to dream that the five days of diarrhea, cramps, vomiting, and everything else involving menstrual difficulties would be compressed into that dream. He told her that she would wake up rested and energetic. Erickson suggested that she would not remember the dream

Two weeks later, she reported to Erickson that she had experienced a cycle without the difficulties that had plagued her since her first menstruation. All of her physical symptoms disappeared. Erickson kept in touch with her for many years, and her problem did not reoccur. This and other healings by Erickson have been documented in medical and scientific literature. Many people believe that hypnosis treats only mental problems or psychosomatic illnesses, not physical illness. This has been proven false.

Erickson suffered from polio as a child. He performed daily self-hypnosis, sometimes lasting hours, just to get out of bed. After gaining a medical degree, he demonstrated that hypnosis could be utilized for numerous physical and mental disorders.

His techniques were creative, exemplified on one occasion by inducing a trance in a Mexican girl who spoke no English. Erickson used hand gestures to induce trance. He once demonstrated to students that trance could be induced by using only three words. But it was his broad use of hypnosis to treat so many illnesses that was most impressive.

In the 1950s, the American Medical Association ended its support for hypnosis as an approved medical modality. Many physiologists and psychiatrists, however, still effectively make use of this technique today. Police utilize it to help witnesses recall license plates, suspects, and possible evidence.

## A PERSONAL EXPERIENCE WITH HYPNOSIS

Jane had a baseball-sized tumor, and it was to be removed the next week. In addition to the tumor, she had two unrelated medical conditions—her heart could stop when she was given anesthesia and she was a bleeder; just drawing a bit of blood for the lab caused her to bleed for many hours. Her ever-present smile vanished.

I told Jane that, if the hospital would allow her to take a tape recorder into surgery, I could create a tape that might help her relax. I was careful to limit her expectations by saying that the tape was primarily for relaxation.

Jane's smile returned. Over the next few days, we had a few hypnosis sessions, during which I showed her the ease and comfort of being in a trance. I had her imagine dry desert sand, and told her the sand could absorb any moisture and control bleeding. She beamed.

The night before her operation, my phone rang. At first, I did not understand what was being said, except that a woman was crying. Finally, I recognized the caller as Jane. The hospital staff refused to allow her to bring the tape to surgery. I reassured her that a copy of the tape existed in her memory, and I instructed her on a method to recall our sessions.

During the operation, Jane experienced minimal bleeding and required only a fraction of the anesthesia normally given. She was released from the hospital early.

Erickson documented many cases of pain control, as well as reduced bleeding, by the use of hypnosis. Not everyone is easily convinced, however. Robert Becker, orthopedic surgeon and former professor of medicine, was skeptical of hypnosis for pain control—at first. He noted, "[I was] afraid…hypnoanalgesia was merely a state in which the patient still felt the pain but didn't respond to it, but [our] experiments proved it was real blockage of pain perception." The experiments he described involved collaboration with another scientist, who used needles to create pain and made electrical measurements of the brain. Becker explains the conclusion of the experiments:

> It seems that the brain can shut off pain by altering the
> direct-current potentials in the rest of the body "at will"…
> by using an innate circuit for attenuating the pain signal,
> which releases a shot of the body's endorphins [internally
> produced opiates].

Although Becker credits the brain, it was the mind causing brain changes that led to opiate production.

Hypnosis can sometimes alleviate pain when drugs fail. I had given workshops on pain control to cancer patients, and held group sessions in my spare time. The results varied. I learned how to detect underlying skepticism, which lowered the chances of any positive effect. As was the case with OCD patients using meditation, motivation and intention are critical to cause real changes in the brain.

As impressive as many of the documented cases of hypnotherapy healings are, there were failures as well. The most limiting feature of hypnotherapy is that even when a patient has had past healings with hypnosis, the next session might not produce any benefit. There could be a variety of physical and mental explanations for this, and many have been suggested in Erickson's and others' publications. Because of this limitation and its negative stigma, hypnotherapy is under-utilized by practitioners.

It should be noted, however, that drugs do not work all the time either. Cancer drugs are heralded as breakthroughs even when they are effective for only a small percent of patients. Also, the body develops resistance to medication so that even though a drug was effective once, it is not guaranteed to be so the next time it is used.

Guided imagery and so-called neurolinguistic programming (NLP) have been employed by therapists whose patients reject hypnosis. Guided imagery produces a trancelike state by having the patient visualize events and scenes that focus the mind. NLP uses words to access memories, resulting in a state of relaxation or even trance. These techniques also depend on the motivation and intention of the patient, and are therefore not 100 percent reliable.

In the previous chapter, we discussed how the mind can affect matter, i.e. the brain. The examples above also show that mind can effect changes in the brain and can trigger cells to activate DNA to produce chemical, mental, and physical changes in the brain and body. Our minds can effect changes either beneficial or harmful to us. One of the ways in which the mind effects such changes has confounded many medical-clinical trials of new drugs.

THE PLACEBO EFFECT

The healing power of the mind has always fascinated me. One especially interesting example of such healing is the so-called placebo effect. According to the *Skeptic's Dictionary*, "The placebo effect is the measurable, observable, or felt improvement in health not attributable to treatment." It goes on to state that this effect is believed by many people to be due to the placebo itself in some mysterious way.

*Placebo* is Latin for "I shall please." It is a medication or treatment believed by the administrator of the treatment to be inert or innocuous. Placebos may be sugar pills or starch pills. Even fake surgery and fake psychotherapy are considered placebos.

In the United States and Western Europe, placebos are often given in clinical trials of candidate drugs in an attempt to show a drug's efficacy. In "double blind" clinical trials, neither the patient nor the physician knows whether the patient is receiving the candidate drug or the placebo.

Only about 5 percent of the candidate drugs that begin clinical trials reach market. The remainder fail, mainly due to safety problems or insufficient efficacy. Nevertheless, for patients, the clinical trials provide hope, and some show significant improvement or even healing with placebos.

Alfred Tauber, professor of medicine and philosophy at Boston University, wrote: "Placebos work, we do not know how, but if scientific medicine is also contaminated with 'bogus' therapies, who is in a position to judge patient satisfaction more than the patient herself?"

One explanation of the placebo effect is that the mind helps facilitate the healing process by thinking the placebo is an aid, when in reality the mind might be generating biochemical events to aid healing.

Margaret Talbot's article "The Placebo Prescription," which appeared in the *New York Times Magazine* on January 9, 2000, described a clinical trial for a procedure that was commonly used for angina forty years earlier. Doctors made small incisions in the chest and tied knots in two arteries to try to increase blood flow to the heart: "It was a popular technique—90% of patients reported it helped—but when [the doctor] compared it with placebo surgery in which he made incisions but did not tie off the arteries, the sham operations proved just as successful." The procedure, known as internal mammary ligation, was eventually abandoned. Still, it showed that the placebo effect occurs even in surgical procedures.

It would not surprise me to find that the placebo effect has had, over the years, more instances of positive effects in clinical-trial patients than the candidate drugs. Instances of patients having miraculous and dramatic reversals of diseases such as cancer provide testimony to the power of self-healing.

The mind can heal. But it also can harm.

## THE NEGATIVE POWER OF SUGGESTION—
## THE NOCEBO EFFECT

The *nocebo* (Latin for "I shall harm") effect can be thought of as the placebo effect's evil shadow. It is an ill effect caused by the suggestion or belief that something is harmful.

One study indicated that patients' expectations that the drug they were taking would have an adverse effect played a significant role in the outcome of the treatment. In other words, patients who thought that the drug would have detrimental side effects experienced significantly more negative reactions to the drug than those who did not believe the drug would have such effects. Author Elizabeth Nobel in her book *Having Twins and More*, describes the negative effects of doctors' comments have on both pregnant women and their unborn children. For example, misdiagnosing a rise in blood pressure (which can be normal in multiple pregnancies) and concluding that a serious condition such as preecampsia exists can result in undue stress on mother and fetus. Such anxiety can lead to premature labor or other complications.

Doctors can unwittingly set negative expectations. It is particularly disturbing to hear of cases in which the patient recovers with the placebo only to be told by the physician that it was a placebo, whereupon the patient relapses and dies.

Negative expectations can even be conveyed while the patient is unconscious. Patients who have undergone deep anesthesia can later recall, under hypnosis, the chatter of the nurses and doctors during an operation. It is sad to learn of cases wherein negative comments concerning chances for recovery were made while the patient was under anesthesia. The compassion that the physician exhibits and the rapport that he builds with the patient are extremely important, especially with serious diseases or operations.

The mind can both heal and harm. What other techniques can help it heal us and improve our lives? One technique used for millennia is meditation.

MEDITATION

Meditation is defined as continuous contemplation on a subject. What can contemplation on a subject accomplish? Deepak Chopra is an endocrinologist and teacher of Vedic traditions. I've attended his workshops and studied his books. According to Vedic teachings, a person can be in one of three different states of consciousness—waking, sleeping, or dreaming. Chopra, however, reminds us that the ancient rishis (or seers) of India taught that a fourth state existed in meditation which transcended ordinary experience. Chopra describes the rishi as:

> a person who has learned to enter the fourth state at will and observe what is there. This ability is not "thinking" as we use the term—the whole phenomenon is an immediate experience, like recognizing the fragrance of lilacs or the sound of a friend's voice. It is immediate, nonverbal, and, unlike a flower's fragrance, totally transforming...In short, the sages observed existence in its purest form.

There are hundreds of methods for meditation. The *Vigyana Bhairava Tantra* lists over 100 different forms of practice. Generally, posture is emphasized; with practice and conditioning, it aids the mind in entering a meditative state. But methods are simply tools.

The meditation technique described in the last chapter is called mindful or focused meditation. This technique teaches a person to hold one thought (such as going to the garden) and allows that thought to be the total reality for that moment. This may seem easy, but most beginning meditators' minds wander to unrelated thoughts that constantly intrude.

What happens once you achieve a state of "meditation," or the fourth state of the *rishis*? Several physiological changes occur: decreased cortisol and adrenaline levels, reduced stress, and improved immune function. A transcendental experience happens for some. How common are such experiences? Polls show that as many as 80 percent of people have had an experience that might be considered transcendental. Author Rita Carter describes transcendental experiences:

> [they] vary enormously…[but contain]certain core  qualities
> which distinguish them from normal consciousness. One is
> the feeling of stillness and freedom from thought, perception
> and anxiety, which nevertheless leaves awareness intact. An-
> other is the sensation of being beyond or outside the physical
> boundaries of the body. A third is ecstasy. And a fourth—per-
> haps the most extraordinary—is a feeling of oneness: loss of
> the usual subject/object divide such that the experiencer be-
> comes what they are experiencing.

Scientists demand evidence, however. Without evidence, meditation is considered to be yet another mumbo-jumbo paranormal phenomenon. Thus, Andrew Newberg, a medical doctor, director of clinical medicine, and assistant professor of radiology, used state-of-the-art methods of examining brain activities by charting the blood flow to specific brain areas. By comparing the scans taken before and during meditation, Newberg and his collaborators were able to show reproducible changes that occur in the brain when one meditates. The scans taken with meditators were very different from those in a "normal" state of mind.

Newberg's study subjects included Tibetan meditators and Franciscan nuns at prayer. There was commonality of brain states with these two groups and the activity of people engaged in spiritual practices.

One area of the brain that decreases in activity during meditation is an area responsible for orientation in physical space. Newburg and his coworkers reasoned that the lack of orientation created some of the effects noted in meditation, but they speculated on another possibility as well. Newberg and his co-authors Eugene D'Aquli and Vince Rause, in their book *Why God Won't Go Away*, wrote when describing the brain scans:

> …we believe that we have colorful evidence on the…com-

puter screen of the brain's capacity to make spiritual experience real. After years of scientific study, and careful consider-
ation of our results, Gene [D'Aquli] and I further believe that
we saw evidence of a neurological process that has evolved
to allow us humans to transcend material existence and acknowledge and connect with a deeper, more spiritual part of
ourselves perceived of as an absolute, universal reality that
connects us to all that is.

This feeling of transcendence is thus documented with an
explanation of how the brain creates the sensation. Here again, we
have documented physical and visual evidence of the mind triggering
the actions of the brain. Does this prove God and the spiritual? No.
Most scientists demand more evidence.

The exact explanation of Newburg's brain scans is not known.
However, the frontal brain areas of the meditation subject are involved.

Another study by Harvard researchers is congruent with Newberg's. Brain imaging provided structural evidence for cortical plasticity (the ability to change the brain's wiring) by showing that the prefrontal cortex is thickened with meditation. This is another validation
of the mind changing brain.

Is there consciousness in meditation? Meditators would generally
say that yes, definitely there is consciousness, but it is like the fourth
mind state that the rishis describe—or mind listening to mind. Though
others meditate in a spiritual but not religious manner, for some of the
religious, meditation can be thought of as prayer. Still, many of those
who pray regard prayer as different from meditation. Prayer is defined
as a reverent petition made to God, or a way to formally establish a
sacred intention.

## PRAYER

As with meditation, there are hundreds of ways to pray. Praying can
be silent or can be accomplished by singing, chanting, quietly speak-

ing, or shouting. The positioning of the hands and body varies. Prayer can be performed even while dancing as the Sufis do. Many religions practice fasting with prayer. "Centering Prayer" was practiced in the sixth century, and it is similar to Eastern meditations in that a single word is repeated like a mantra: for example, the word could be "love," "Jesus," or "peace." As with meditation, prayer is the method or means by which to achieve a specific state of mind.

George Gallup, Jr. has conducted numerous polls on prayer. Regarding Americans, Gallop reports in his year 2000 audit:

> [nine in ten] pray and believe in the power of prayer …A remarkable three persons in ten report instance of a profound healing of a physical, emotional, or spiritual nature. This proportion projects to sixty million adults…Many who pray seek a closer link between the medical and spiritual worlds…only six percent of…their doctors pray for them…Among those who experience a doctor praying with them, as many as 93 percent think the doctor's prayer helped them with their medical problems.

In addition to the evidence of brain changes reported by Newberg's study of Franciscan nuns at prayer, other studies show the healing power of prayer. Larry Dossey, a medical doctor, internist, and author, reports that over 130 controlled laboratory studies indicate that prayer or prayer-like states result in positive health changes in humans and other living organisms.

## COMMONALITY OF HYPNOSIS, MEDITATION, GUIDED IMAGERY, AND PRAYER

What do all of these techniques do? Properly performed, hypnosis, meditation, guided imagery, and prayer all quiet the normally noisy, thinking brain. Any of these techniques can be performed alone or with a therapist.

One can think of hypnosis and guided imagery as goal-oriented, attempting to heal, access memories (or core features of mental make-up), treat diseases, or deal with undesirable emotions.

What I observe when people pray or meditate is that these processes place their minds in a "quiet" state. I come to this conclusion from observations of their faces and their body language. As a hypnotherapist, I have learned to recognize trance from facial and bodily changes. I find it remarkable that, no matter the individual's religious or spiritual beliefs, this "quieting" of the mind is a commonality.

Can it be that this state is accessed in all religions and in all forms of spirituality? I believe the answer is yes. Whatever this state is, one of the reasons people embrace spirituality is the transcendence that accompanies it. I think most religions have served humankind well by providing this tool, by teaching this mode to access the spiritual.

There are numerous reports of healing due to the action of group meditation and prayer. Researchers in Transcendental Meditation have conducted experiments in attempts to reduce crime and improve communities. Successes were found, and group meditation was shown more effective than meditation of single individuals. Physician Rex Gardner reported on the case of a woman with a severe ulcerous varicose condition on her leg. He had told her that even if she were healed by medication or surgery, the scar would require skin grafting. Her church group prayed for her. A day after the prayer meeting, complete healing occurred and no grafting was required. Gardner reported:

> [the story is] so bizarre the I would not have included it [in my report] had I not been one of the doctors who examined the patient's leg at the next monthly prayer meeting and had all the people who had been present not been available for interrogation.

Was her healing caused by prayer, or was this a placebo effect? The validity of such group studies is inconclusive due to the lack of control groups.

THE POWER OF LOVE

One essential component in all healing is love and compassion. In the last century, Western medicine has developed a so-called standard of care. Unfortunately, this usually involves a defined process for diagnosis and treatment that leaves care and love out of the standard. The results of the Gallup poll mentioned earlier indicate that over 90 percent of patients long for care and love from their doctors.

"Love" has many possible meanings. I define love as deep affection for a person or persons, resulting in an attachment and a sense of oneness. "Oneness" is consistent with the upixels that are all interconnected through nonlocality.

Such deep affection can be for one's self. Loving the self is essential in healing. Self-image can be an aid or impediment in healing. Bernie Siegel, a medical doctor, believes that unconditional love is a powerful resource for our immune systems. Siegel's workshops and books present convincing evidence that love is essential in both spiritual healing and self-healing. When I attended one of his workshops, we made sketches depicting ourselves. It was interesting to see the sketches from AIDS and cancer patients. Dark colors and hunched-over bodies revealed depression and pessimism, while vibrant colors and scenes of figures enjoying nature reflected hope and optimism.

The mind can heal or harm. Love, or the absence of it, wields a powerful influence over the mind and body. Siegel points out a study that followed college students through midlife. Those from loving families had only a 29 percent significant disease rate while those who did not had a 95 percent chance of some major illness.

Numerous studies have shown how love produces electrochemical action in the brain, which, in turn, produces chemicals that strengthen the immune system. Dean Ornish, a cardiologist, has reported clinical studies involving patients suffering from arteriosclerosis and angina. These studies indicate that love, or the absence of love, directly impacts the seriousness of the disease as well as the odds for survival.

Physician Eugene Straus and author Alex Straus listed the top 100 medical advances in history. They remind us that the most important one—compassionate healthcare—was realized over several centuries at different times by different cultures:

> ...the single greatest advance in the history of medicine...is the movement away from an approach to the sick that was characterized by shunning and abandonment, toward one in which the sufferer is fed, protected, and nurtured like a child. Without this most basic concept...nothing is medically possible.

In other words, despite modern wonders of medicine, the greatest medical advancement was moving from fear to love.

## HOW DO HYPNOSIS, MEDITATION, LOVE, AND PRAYER WORK?

We explored a model in Chapter 7, Figure 1 as to how mind and consciousness connect to the information realm. Do our minds and consciousness access the information realm during meditation and prayer? It is the mind that produces changes in the brain, which in turn affects our state of health with positive and negative results. Intention, thought, and belief cause the upixels' actions. Resulting signals spread throughout the brain and body, leading to healing. Therefore, it is the unconscious, the conscious, and the mind that allow healing in hypnosis, meditation, and prayer. Such change can be detected at the cellular level, with action on DNA that results in permanent physical and mental changes.

Could it be that our noisy brains are so intent on grasping and processing a billionth of the 4 percent of the universe that we ignore the other messages of the universe's upixels? It is tempting to speculate that the upixels contain so much information that quieting the brain/mind accesses wisdom beyond normal human consciousness. The collective unconscious that Jung postulated might be a phenomenon of accessing the wisdom in the universe's upixels, or even the information realm that instructs the upixels.

## THE HEALING MIND

Our world is space filled with energy. What are we then? The body, the brain, and the mind are a result of energy. The mind creates our reality from the information of the universe. Where is the mind? If the "mind" of a TV is the energy waves that create the program, then our mind is everywhere since all energy and all upixels are interconnected. The upixels, which are out there and in us, initiate the physical process in the brain. And, as we will learn in the next chapter, we radiate mind/energy into the universe.

Although humans have spent billions of dollars developing new drugs, harnessing the power of the atom, and sending men and women into space, we have not learned how to utilize the power of our own minds. To do so will require nonmaterial perspectives that involve practices such as meditation, spirituality, and prayer. There is strong evidence for the mind as a healer, but this force has not yet been integrated into medicine and healthcare.

If quantum entities are connected on a nonlocal level in the information realm and the mind arises from this realm, are minds connected on a nonlocal level too? Are thoughts and intentions connected in a nonlocal fashion through quantum interactions instantly communicated between minds? If so, this would be a scientific explanation of the collective power of prayer or meditation. Following this line of reasoning, could such concerted intention and free will reshape our future, not only on the personal level but also on the societal?

The power of the atom used to create electricity comes not from a single atom but from many billions of atoms acting together. Similarly, the power of the human brain can be fully utilized when we learn to use this great force in unity with many.

This brings us to spiritual and religious beliefs. Our minds might be accessing the information realm during meditation and prayer. Is this a spiritual realm? Can the rift between science and spirituality be reconciled with this insight?

> *During the past thirty years, people from all civilized countries of the earth have consulted me. I have treated many hundreds of patients…Protestants…Jews…It is safe to say that every one of them fell ill because he had lost that which the living religions of every age have given to their followers, and none of them has really been healed who did not regain his religious outlook.*
>
> –Carl G. Jung

> *Doctors don't know everything really. They understand matter, not spirit. And you and I live in the spirit.*
>
> –William Saroyan

# HEALING THE RIFT

# 9

# SPIRITUALITY, RELIGION, AND SCIENCE

*Every concept of God is a mere simulacrum, a false likeness, an idol: it could not reveal God himself.*

−Gregory of Nyssa

I recall seeing an old faded photograph of my Uncle Johnny as a young man standing in front of an airplane with several other young men. Uncle Johnny had served in World War II as a tail gunner, but he never spoke of the war. A quiet man, he said little to me as I was growing up. What I knew of his past, I learned from my mother. She said that many missions resulted in Johnny's plane being bullet-riddled as it sputtered back to the airbase. Many in his air squadron were killed in action. Others were captured and served out the remainder of the war in German POW camps. But the photograph revealed none of that—just smiling young airmen as they stood in front of an airplane.

A few years after Doris died, I learned that Uncle Johnny was dying of colon cancer. During my drive to visit him at a hospital near my parents' home, I had mixed emotions. Each visit to the small town in the Central Valley of California triggered memories of my youth that I kept shut in a closet of my mind. I did not feel comfortable seeing a relative dying of cancer. I'd seen too many suffering from this disease in the last few years.

To my surprise, Johnny not only looked happy, he was happy. The opposite of any cancer patient I'd ever seen. He was happy not just to see me, but happy with himself and the world. I knew that he'd become religious, and I wondered if this was the reason for his happiness.

Looking at me with intense eyes and a smile, he said in a calm, matter-of-fact way, "Everybody dies." That put me at ease. He then recounted the awakening he'd experienced with religion. For the first time, he told me of his war years and his subsequent search for the meaning of life. Johnny described how he became religious in the last few decades, concluding by saying, "I found God."

Johnny had told his story to all the nurses and staff at the hospital, yet they gathered around to hear it again. It was told with a loving tone. Having seen many cancer patients, I knew that he was in pain. Although his wasted body revealed terminal illness, his attitude and voice conveyed a different message. Johnny said that he wanted everyone to feel comfortable with his passing and that he was ready to move on. He died two days later.

Driving home the day of our visit, I realized that I felt better than I did before the visit, something that I never would have predicted. Johnny was so happy; I wondered what I was missing. Several of the nurses told me that he was an exceptional patient. They explained that, as difficult as their job was, he made them feel positive about their roles. They said that they had never witnessed such calm and peace.

I thought once again about the nature of reality. What might I be missing from the spiritual and religious realms?

## REALITY IS BEYOND OUR COMPREHENSION

We have discussed science's theories of our beginnings, existence, and reality. Now, let's review spiritual and religious perspectives.

Spiritual and religious teachings generally agree that we humans cannot comprehend reality, which usually includes God. In general, religions teach that God and mystical reality are different from what we experience in ordinary consciousness.

Jesus, according to the Gnostic script Gospel of Thomas 113, said

"The kingdom of the Father is spread out upon the Earth, and men do not see it." Buddhists believe that it is impossible to understand the world through our senses, philosophies, or science. Judaism agrees that we cannot comprehend God. The Sufis of Islam teach that metaphors and symbols cannot reveal the divine. According to Hinduism, maya is the illusion of reality in which we live. Taoism and Confucianism, although in many ways different, both hold that reality is beyond human comprehension.

## SCIENCE, RELIGIONS, AND SPIRITUALITY USE METAPHORS

Since the comprehension of reality is so seemingly impossible, humans are reduced to using metaphors to describe our world. Joseph Campbell, a 20th-century author and professor of mythology, studied ancient myths and their similarities to religious teachings. Campbell wrote that, long before there was writing or widespread literacy, myth was the means of imparting knowledge. An essential ingredient and tool of myth is metaphor. Campbell claimed that many religious conflicts were created by the failure to appreciate that religious writings were metaphorical and should not be taken literally.

Religions and spiritual teachings rarely change their metaphors. Indeed, the schisms within the major religions that led to conflicting factions have been due, at least in part, to the desire to change some metaphor in the religion's teachings. Alfred Whitehead, the great American mathematician whose father was an Anglican clergyman, wrote that religion will not regain its old power until it can embrace change in the same spirit as science. He felt its principles might be eternal, but the expression of those principles requires continual development.

One difference between scientific and religious teachings is that science is constantly revising its metaphors. Scientists understand that their theories are but metaphors, and this results in the continual search for better ones. As Einstein said, "No amount of experimentation can ever prove me right; a single experiment can prove me wrong," among different religions and cultures. Multiple gods were recognized in ancient Greece. Monotheism, or the belief in only one God, developed with Judaism, Christianity, and Islam. Christianity teaches the Trinity or the three aspects of God—the Father and creator God, the Son Jesus, and the Holy Spirit. Islam recognizes only one God, but both Moses and Jesus are regarded as holy men and prophets. Hinduism teaches there was no beginning to the universe, yet it has many gods, including gods of creation and gods of destruction. The original Buddhism had a multiplicity of gods, but many current forms of Buddhism avoid the word "god." Taoism does not use a god as the highest truth; Confucius, although not excluding the possibility of the existence of spirits, did not refer to a god who governed good and evil.

How do all these diverse beliefs in God affect the spiritual? Religions have taught that expectations, scientific concepts, notions of reality, ideas about God, ego, and personality all block our ability to know the reality of the spirit. Is science's information realm an apt metaphor for spirit? If our bodies' and brains' actions are the result of mind, which is connected to the information realm in a nonlocal fashion, then the information realm might be regarded as spiritual. Spiritual individuals believe spirit is an animating or vital principle that gives life to physical organisms. Indeed, Figure 1 in Chapter 7 indicates that mind/consciousness conveys the vital principle to our brains and bodies. Matthew Fox wrote that spirit is in the soul but is greater than the soul:

> Spirit is everyone's and no one's. No one possesses spirit, it's
> not private property. No church owns it; no religion owns it.
> It's greater than the soul. Spirit requires receptivity, an open
> heart, a letting go.

What metaphor might give us insight into this immaterial essence that makes up the spiritual?

From a scientific perspective, information acting on upixels is such a metaphor. From a spiritual perspective, the energy metaphor of Eastern and Western traditions—that everything is energy—is consistent with upixels and quantum theory.

## ENERGY AND LIFE

Energy is the capacity for acting. The universe consists of energy of different types and frequencies. Humans, for example, generate energy fields at various frequencies. Humans are also affected emotionally, cognitively, and behaviorally by electromagnetic energy fields that exist in our environment.

For decades, scientists, healers, and spiritual followers have studied energy in the human body. But energy concepts are thousands of years old, as in the Vedic and Hindu teachings of energy points (or chakras). These ancient traditions recognize that energy is located in bodily "energy centers." The *Kabbalah*, a Jewish mystical philosophy, also recognizes such energy and calls it *nefish*. Christian teachings have numerous references to energy as life. In Hindu, *Kundalini* is life's energy and can be utilized for a spiritual awakening. *Reiki*, a hands-on healing method, is derived from various Buddhist teachings; in Japanese, it means "spiritually guided life-force energy."

Author Paul Pearsall reminds us of the Polynesian belief in energy:

> ...more than 2,000 years ago, there existed a people who lived in paradise...They did not live apart from the universe but saw themselves as infinitely evolving manifestations of manna (energy) of a living universe. For them there was no death, only transitions to various unfolding embodiments of the vibrant energy and information that was their spirit and soul...Every chant...(prayer) represented their confidence that they and everyone and everything they loved were forever energetically connected, alive, and evolving.

Australian aboriginals, whose culture goes back 60,000 years, believe in "dreamtime" or tjukurpa—that there is no separation of man and nature, of life and death, or of past, present, and future. Their music unites consciousness with the energy patterns of nature. Bantu, a traditional African religion, believes that life is force or muntu—a vital energy endowed with intelligence and will. Followers believe that the dead have deeper knowledge of the forces and interact with the living. Native Americans believe in a dynamic energy system in which all systems of nature are one, communicating and interacting. Mesoamerican religions—Maya, Zapitec, Mixtec, and Aztec—all had a concept of a vital force or energy in all life.

The world's cultures and religions have recognized that energy is life's vital force. Scientists also acknowledge that energy runs through our bodies. This energy produces an energy field, or what some call the "human energy field." But what evidence exists to support ancient concepts of energy centers and chakras, or beliefs that we are one with nature? Scientists expect reproducible experiments and data to support such claims.

## MEASURING THE HUMAN ENERGY FIELD

As we've previously discussed, humans generate electromagnetic energy that can be measured using ECGs for heart functions and EEGs for brain functions. All living multicellular organisms produce an electrical current and an associated electrical field, or energy field. Valerie Hunt, a physical therapist and professor of kinesiology at UCLA, utilized a machine called an "electromyograph" to measure electrical activity in the muscles. While the typical electrical frequency in brain activity is between about 0-30 cps (cycles per second), muscle energy frequencies are about 225 cps, and the heart clocks in at about 250 cps.

Hunt found a much weaker yet verifiable electrical field outside the body, with frequencies ranging between a hundred and 1,600 cp Spatially, these fields of energy were better correlated with the chakras than with any organs, thus providing scientific evidence for the ancient Hindu and Chinese teachings about energy fields.

The Hindu and Chinese, as well as many other ancient cultures, believed that the flow of energy in the body dictates the degree of our well-being. Is there scientific evidence to support this conclusion in the same manner by which scientific evidence has supported the existence of energy fields?

## WHAT CAN AFFECT THE HUMAN ENERGY FIELD?

Hunt noticed that the environment affected the human energy field. In Southern California, for example, the easterly Santa Ana winds, which carry strong positive ions, would cause the human energy field to become smaller. Inversely, the energy field expanded near the sea and across the mountains, possibly due to increased negative ions. Hunt utilized a specially-built room that could alter the normal electromagnetic energy of the air as well as the magnetic features of the room. The results were dramatic.

When the electromagnetism was reduced, people's energy fields were weakened, and the subjects in the room reacted by crying. When the energy field was increased above the normal level, people reported clear thinking and expanded consciousness. When the electrical conditions were normal but the level of magnetism decreased, the people suffered gross loss of coordination. This study is evidence that we are, indeed, one with nature. We are intimately connected to it, are affected by it, and affect it ourselves through our own energy fields.

I have discussed how the mind can aid the body's healing. Hunt has suggested that her energy findings might lead to treatment options for several diseases, including cerebral palsy, multiple sclerosis, and Lou Gehrig's disease. What would cause her to think this? What evidence exists to support energy healing?

Broken bones heal by growing tissues to connect and bind the fracture. Physician Robert Becker found that applying electrical energy at 8 cps to fractures and injuries increases the rate of healing. Becker began his research with salamanders and later with frogs. Using various metals as electrodes, especially silver electrodes, he and his coworkers were able to heal fractured bones in humans with electrical energy.

Becker suggests that the healing is started with electrical energy initiating a network of chemical reactions. First, the energy acts on the cell membrane that releases chemicals that act at the DNA level, influencing which genes are turned on. The cells that are appropriately "turned on" result in the binding of the fractured bone—thus, healing. Although this rationale for the mode of action was speculation, energy bone-healings were demonstrated on numerous patients.

We know that the mind can heal and cause changes at the DNA level. We also know that electrical energy appropriately applied to fractured bones can heal them.

What is the explanation? In 2006, seventeen scientists in the United States, Europe, and Asia reported that human skin cells produce their own electric fields and that these fields provide directional cues for cell movement during healing. Specific genes were identified that responded to electric fields. This research explains why applied electrical energy aids the healing of wounds and, perhaps, the healing of broken bones.

LIFE—BROADCASTING AND RECEIVING ENERGY

The ability to produce electrical energy probably began with first life. The bags that create life's energy by pumping protons, such as mitochondria, are arranged in complex networks in humans producing several energy fields. These energy fields operate at various frequencies and extend both within and outside the body, corresponding to Eastern beliefs concerning bodily energy centers.

Additional evidence is cited by William Tiller, who found that all life emits photons. A scientist and the author of *Science and Human*

*Transformations*, Tiller discussed several studies of photon emission from various living organisms, including humans:

> Ultra-weak photon emission from various living systems is a common phenomenon for all plants and animals with the radiation intensity being on the order of a few hundred to a few thousand photons per second. For mammalian cells, this has been estimated to be about 1 photon per cell in 3-20 minutes.

These results, and related evidence for such light or energy emissions, have been published in numerous scientific journals. Humans create and radiate light of various frequencies. I disclosed in earlier chapters that light becomes entangled and communicates instantly through nonlocality via the information realm. Here, we have a possible connection to the information realm.

We know that humans radiate energy. What about the energy of the universe affecting humans?

As described earlier in her studies of human energy fields, Hunt found that external electromagnetic energy affects human emotions, thinking, and coordination. The human body and brain, in addition to broadcasting their energy, are also receivers of upixels from the electrical fields of the environment. These affect brain and bodily functions. Just as radio reception is disrupted near power lines, external electromagnetic energy, such as the positive ions mentioned by Hunt, can adversely affect the human energy field and our brain's receiver. An increase in the human energy field can result in clear thinking and expanded consciousness just as a strong signal from a TV station results in clear reception.

We generate energy that radiates into the information realm, and we receive and are influenced by energy from the universe. This suggests that mind and consciousness, which are connected to the information realm, direct the upixels. We also learned that quantum-brain advocates believe that the quantum events occur in microtubules within our neurons. These processes in neurons result in the brain revealing the information of mind and consciousness supplied by the upixels.

As discussed previously in this chapter, the ancients taught that reality was beyond comprehension. They also believed that energy was the vital force. Scientists now realize that our world is energy transformed by information.

## MATERIALISM—DIGRESSION FROM REALITY

Although I have emphasized that materialism is a principal cause of spirituality's rift with science, I would like to review again why materialism became our paradigm for reality.

About the time of Isaac Newton, scientists began to explain our world with theories based on mathematics. Like magic, these theories predicted the outcome of experiments and observations. Then the atom was discovered and, later, the components of atoms. Even then, metaphors and similes made scientific concepts understandable. One of the popular metaphors: our world is composed entirely of billiard ball-like entities. Atoms and their constituent electrons, protons, and neutrons were represented with billiard ball-type models. This was the beginning of materialism, i.e. the belief that all reality is material.

Scientific discoveries led to technological contributions such as the steam engine, automobile, and airplane. All of these materialistic wonders transformed our world and lifestyle. Increasingly, materialism became the primary focus of both society and scientists in the Western world.

## THE BEGINNING OF THE RIFT

Although "immaterial" discoveries were made, such as electricity (the flow of electrons) and X-rays, they were difficult for laypeople and even scientists to fully understand. Much of the early days of electricity had Tesla coils exhibited as a paranormal phenomenon and entertainment. Even X-rays were used as a novelty to dazzle the public by exposing the bones of fully clothed people.

Anything immaterial was more difficult to grasp. Thus, during the 19th and 20th centuries, the public and nearly all scientists increasingly agreed that reality was based upon material entities such as atoms. This is still the prevailing concept of reality. Though many spiritual individuals also believe that reality is material, they also believe that somewhere "out there" is the spiritual. In other words, our everyday world is only material, but the creation of our world and death somehow involves the spiritual.

### EMERGING TRUTH

Beginning in the early 20th century, a new concept of reality, quantum theory, emerged. The quantum world consisted of highly complex mathematical equations that baffled even scientists. Several strange concepts were proposed to explain quantum theory's meaning. However, even the founders of the theory could not agree upon which concept was correct.

Except for theoretical physicists and electrical engineers who used the theory (but did not understand its meaning) as the basis for radio, television, and other electrical devices, scientists saw little practical value in quantum theory. These scientists had little exposure to quantum theory other than college introductory courses. Most students despised or avoided these courses. As a profound truth, quantum theory lurked in the background—that is, until the 21st century.

### A MOVE BACK TO THE SPIRITUAL

The movement to such truth began with a handful of early 20th-century physicists, who became increasing philosophical and even spiritual in their attempts to understand the revelations of quantum theory. Sir James Hopwood Jeans, a great mathematician, physicist, and cosmologist, said:

When we view ourselves in space and time, our conscious-
nesses are obviously the separate individuals of a particle-
picture, but when we pass beyond space and time, they may
perhaps form ingredients of a single continuous stream of life.
As it is with light and electricity, so it may be with life; the
phenomena may be individuals carrying on separate existenc-
es in space and time, while in the deeper reality beyond space
and time, we may all be members of one body.

I have discussed space and time and how our perceptions of both
do not portray reality. Quantum theory suggests that what is really
"out there" is immaterial. Immaterial energy, including dark energy
and the energy of the vacuum, is becoming the new reality. I stated
earlier that physicists believe the universe is immaterial, mental, and
spiritual. This view of a spiritual world and immaterial reality is shared
by increasing numbers of scientists in the 21st century. It is a concept
taught by virtually all cultures for thousands of years. In his essay in the
prestigious journal *Nature* in 2005, Richard Henry, professor of physics and astronomy at John Hopkins University, explains:

Physicists shy from the truth because the truth is so alien
to everyday physics…the wave function is collapsed [into a
particle] simply by your human mind seeing nothing…One
benefit of switching humanity to a correct perception of the
world is the resulting joy of discovering the mental nature
of the Universe… Beyond the acquisition of this perception,
physics can no longer help.

This new "truth" is a modern rationale for an ancient concept.
Henry shares my view of sight, that we see nothing. He also believes
that our perceptions are merely the result of the brain receiving information contained in light, and our consciousness creates the "matter"
when upixels collapse into "particles." Thus, the universe is mental. If
physics can no longer help, perhaps spirituality can. Because of materialism, scientists and the public digressed into a cul-de-sac off the path

of the spiritual. But the collective unconscious appears to be emerging regardless.

Consider the teachings of 2,000 years ago as related by physicist Russell Targ and spiritual healer Jane Katra in their book, *Miracles of the Mind*:

> Patanjali, the Hindu philosopher and Sanskrit writer of the Yorga Sutras…taught that we obtain psi [psychic] data by accessing what has become known as the Akashic records, the aspect of nonlocal mind that contains all information past, present, and future [collective unconscious]. One accesses it, he said, by 'becoming it,' with a single mental tool kit to accomplish this. Patanjali tells us that in order to see the world in our mind, we must quiet our mental activity.

I have suggested that, during meditation and prayer, our minds access the information realm where nonlocality and all information of the past, present, and future reside. The Hindus knew all this 2,000 years ago.

As Targ and Katra remind us, 2,000 years ago the ancients used a spiritual perspective to consider the upixels of the universe. They taught that all times are locked away and available to us. Patanjali reminded us that the key to the lock is a quiet mind created by meditation and prayer. Is access to the collective unconscious behind that locked door?

We find in this chapter that spiritual leaders from different times and places had similar metaphors for reality. These included life's vital essence being energy, the flow of such energy in bodily energy fields, and beliefs in the spiritual nature of our world. How could the ancient mystics have discovered truths that scientists are just now beginning to accept? Did they access the information realm through meditation and prayer?

The scientific studies of Newberg and others (discussed in Chapter 8) indicate a different kind of brain state during meditation and prayer.

The phenomenon is reproducible. The mystical wisdom and "spiritual truths" discovered by all cultures and summarized in this chapter provide reproducible results.

However, to heal the rift between science and spirituality, scientists demand an explanation or a scientific metaphor.

## AN EXPLANATION: INFORMATION AND UPIXELS

Energy is what we experience as our world and reality. Energy—the upixels—may come from the vacuum, from other dimensions, or from other universes. Consciousness and mind direct the action and changes in the brain and body through the upixels. Like a radio broadcast, humans generate information and an energy field forever permeating the universe. The energy mingles with the released light from the Big Bang which is still inundating us from every direction.

The energy waves of the universe engulf us in information, and we radiate selected responses. The energy we receive and radiate, as well as the energy which becomes "us" for an instant, is but waves. We conceive ourselves as localized beings of certain physical dimensions that possess consciousness, yet the mind and consciousness result from the universe's wholeness. All the energy overwhelming us with information, all the information we radiate, and all the upixels that becomes "us" are mind and consciousness.

How does this fit with the concept that all possible events are out there? Collectively, we all place events into our universe from infinite possibilities. Our world is the result of the oscillations we choose and create from the abyss. Every thought, action, and emotion is recorded in our universe.

Therefore, we are energy, and we are dependent upon the energy around us. The energy that makes up our vital essence and everything in the universe is interconnected at the upixel level. Cultures, religions, and teachings worldwide have known this for thousands of years— that we are all one. Here, science and spirituality agree. The wholeness concept of physics suggested by nonlocality also holds that we are one with the universe. The great 20th-century physicist Werner Heisenberg said: "After the experiences of modern physics, our attitude towards concepts like mind or the human soul or life or God will be different."

The Oxford theologian Keith Ward, when speaking of opposites in God such as the trinity and unity, used an analogy with quantum theory, "they are not contradictions, but inadequate attempts to articulate the Divine nature, which we cannot grasp in itself, like the wave-particle duality in physics... they have a consistent application in fact."

Man's metaphors to describe our world are generally inadequate. This is a concept that spirituality has known for thousands of years. The best metaphor of our universe from science is that it is made of energy. Again, we find an ancient metaphor. Scientists believe in an information realm where all of the past, present, and future exist. Humans have been accessing this realm with meditation and prayer for millennia. Upixels are the means of expressing mind and consciousness to brain and body. Upixels also connect us to everything in the universe through the information realm and nonlocality. Recognizing that reality is immaterial empowers scientists with the rationale to embrace the spiritual.

## WISDOM AND ENERGY

We are generally focused on the world of our own experiences, but when we manage to quiet the thinking receiver/processor brain, we access self-healing and deep wisdom. This access arises somehow from the upixels, because upixels are messengers of the information realm via our mind and consciousness. How do we access archetypal wisdom? If all times are out there, and mind and consciousness create reality, then perhaps we should not worry about the definition of first life. Rather, we should ponder who or what created mind and consciousness. Can science address this? Perhaps, in the final analysis, only spirituality is qualified to address how our world of mind/consciousness was created.

All of this puts a perspective on life and death. Since we are the result of the Big Bang, energy, information, and a timeless reality in which all events are possible, who or what was born and who or what dies? What happens when we die? If the energy of the dead is still out there, is it possible to communicate with the dead?

> *We do not know how the scientists of the next century will define energy or in what strange jargon they will discuss it. But no matter what language the physicists use, they will not come into contradiction with Blake. Energy will remain in some sense the lord and giver of life, a reality transcending our mathematical descriptions. Its nature lies at the heart of the mystery of our existence as animate beings in an inanimate universe.*

> –Freeman Dyson

> *Energy is the only life...as Reason is the boundary or outward circumference of Energy.*

> –William Blake

# 10
# AFTERLIFE

*A free man thinks of nothing less than death, and his widom is
meditation not of death but of life.*

–Benedict de Spinoza

Goodbyes can stir up buried memories. My farewell to Josie was no exception. A former seamstress, Josie dressed in immaculately tailored clothes. With her radiant smile, she always appeared as though she'd just emerged from a beauty parlor. Her home would have passed for an "open house" showcased by realtors and in it she helped her large immigrant family stay close by hosting many dinner parties.

Anyone who knew her this way would have been surprised to find out that Josie had cancer. She and my brother managed to keep it a secret from the family for almost five years. During this time, my older sister's husband died of complications from cancer. Perhaps the family's grief over his illness and death was part of the reason for Josie's secrecy.

The last time I saw her, she looked thin, and my brother said that she was on a diet. About nine months later, I learned that she had terminal cancer. She'd rejected medication and radiation therapy due to the side effects and the inevitability of the outcome.

Josie died on their 38th wedding anniversary. During her final days, she spoke of angels and heaven.

At her funeral, the minister discussed the celebration of life and the reality of heaven. I was reminded of Stanley's funeral decades earlier and similar words about heaven. The service was a beautiful celebration of Josie's life, enlivened by many biblical quotations and culminating in a slide show of images of her as a baby, a young girl, a bride, and a mother. The background music of Sarah Brightman and Andrea Bocelli singing "Time to Say Goodbye" served to strengthen the impact of the photographic essay of Josie's well-lived life.

The grief of the moment opened the closet that contained the latent feelings for all my family and friends who'd died—my parents, Uncle Johnny, Stanley, and Doris. All of these emotions were transformed into a flood of tears—enough for all of them.

Josie left behind a husband, a daughter, a grandson, and three siblings, all of whom seemed comforted by religion and their belief of heaven. But is the belief in an afterlife simply a way for humans to accept death and make it more bearable?

Most people want to believe there is something positive that follows what we call "death." Materialists, on the other hand, would contend that nothing survives death. Most Westerners believe in materialistic versions of science, while also believing in some form of spirituality. Thus, the question of an afterlife is a central issue in reconciling the differences between science and spirituality.

AGELESS MYSTERY: AFTER DEATH, WHAT WILL WE BECOME?

We live in a false reality. With our seeming inability to directly perceive reality, how can we really pretend to know what we are, let alone know what will happen to us after death? It seems illogical to jump to the conclusion that nothing survives death, since reality itself is so elusive.

But in asking the question, what is death, we are also asking, what is life? If life is energy, what happens to that energy when we die?

Is death a myth? Of those who believe in an afterlife, about half believe in reincarnation, while the remainder believe in a shift to another place such as heaven. At first glance, these appear to be quite different metaphors. However, both are included in *The Tibetan Book of the Dead*, which teaches that a given soul or spirit can achieve different states after death, and only one involves reincarnation. After death, if the soul recognizes the clear light of consciousness (*Dharmakaya*), it becomes free and no longer needs to be involved with reincarnation. This level might be equated with heaven. Only if the soul misses the opportunities of light or the light of peaceful gods does the soul become reincarnated. In a similar manner, Hinduism teaches of two possible paths to take after death: one to the gods and one to the Earth.

Christianity and Judaism subscribed to a form of reincarnation until about the fourth century after Christ. Therefore, one cannot make black-and-white generalizations, such as that Christians do not believe in reincarnation or Buddhists do not believe in heaven. It depends on the particular teachings.

Can spirit, energy, or upixels give us clues to an afterlife? Yes, they can. Additional evidence of energy being our essence is supplied by individuals who have experienced so-called near-death experiences or communication with the dead or dying.

In the second half of the 20th century, "after-death," "out-of-body," and "near-death" were terms coined to describe the phenomenon of people who were already declared clinically dead yet recovered. Many of them could relate their experiences during the short time in which they were dead. So, to understand death, we take some additional perspective from the accounts of those who have actually "died."

## WHAT IS DEATH?

Dannion Brinkley was talking on the phone on the night of September 17, 1975. He said, "Hey, Tommy, I've got to get going, a storm's coming."

Tommy said, "So what?"

"Tommy, I gotta go. Mother always told me never to talk on the phone during a thunderstorm."

As Brinkley described later, "The next sound I heard was like a freight train coming into my ear at the speed of light." He was struck by lightning. The nails of his shoes were welded to the nails in the floor. He was thrown into the air, minus his shoes. Brinkley then described what he experienced:

> From immense pain I found myself engulfed by peace and tranquility. It was a feeling I had never known before and have not had since. It was like bathing in a glorious calmness.

CPR brought Brinkley back to consciousness, but he slipped away. Later, he described how he could view his body with shoeless feet from fifteen feet above everyone in his house. The medical technician declared Brinkley "gone." Brinkley described the sensation of next entering a tunnel and moving toward a brilliant light.

During the time that Brinkley was "gone," his body was placed into an ambulance. During the ride to the hospital the heart monitor was flat—he had no heartbeat. At the hospital his body was taken to the emergency room and resuscitation efforts were made. Adrenalin was injected directly into his heart. Still, no response. Electrical paddles were applied as well as additional CPR attempts. The heart monitor remained flat. The attending doctor informed Brinkley's wife that her husband was dead.

Brinkley was on a gurney headed for the morgue when someone noticed that the sheet covering his face was moving. He was breathing.

Brinkley was totally transformed by his near-death experience. He took a much more spiritual path afterward. He claimed to have gained certain knowledge of energy, and became obsessed with creating an electronic device to help people access the spiritual realm.

This is one account of a so-called near-death experience, or NDE. What exactly is death then? "Clinically dead" refers to a person having no pulse or heartbeat and no respiration. Yet, at least for a while, biochemical reactions are still occurring in the tissues and organs and in the membrane bags pumping protons.

A more conservative definition of death is the permanent cessation of all vital functions and the loss of brain stem and spinal reflexes, as well as flat EEGs over at least 24 hours. However, these elaborate tests are rarely performed in a rigorous fashion, and most deaths are declared after respiration and the heartbeat cease.

P.M.H. Atwater, who "died" three times, wrote several books on near-death experiences. She contends that researchers have been reluctant to associate near-death with full death. What about the general public? George Gallup Jr. and William Proctor co-authored a book titled *Adventures in Immortality*, which was published in 1982. They reported that their survey revealed that eight million Americans had undergone NDEs, and about 100 million Americans believed that life existed beyond death.

## HE DIED TWICE AND LIVED TO TELL THE TALE

In 1994, Brinkley's book, *Saved by the Light*, was published. His memoir described two near-death experiences. As indicated previously, he was struck by lightning and was clinically dead. Years later, he suffered heart complications and experienced a similar death, which was followed by recovery. One could take issue with the interpretations of his experiences while clinically dead, but several of his descriptions are illuminating.

I found it most interesting that Brinkley became interested in electronics and had several electronic businesses after his "first death." He describes his obsessive interest in the energy that appeared in his visions. He began to realize certain things about the human body:

> We transmit spiritual, mental, and physical essences of ourselves to the world around us...When you reach the point where you can control this energy and transform it into positive force, you have found the part of you that is God.

### THREE DEATH EXPERIENCES, THEN 3,000 MORE

P.M.H. Atwater, in her book, *Beyond the Light*, described her three "deaths" in 1977. Although these were not verified by medical records because she was not hospitalized, a medical specialist agreed that she had died. In her quest to understand her experiences, she interviewed over 3,000 people who'd experienced NDEs. Frequently mentioned were cases of extrasensory perception, including the ability to know the future after the NDE.

Those who underwent near-death experiences gained a remarkable electromagnetic sensitivity. This included sensitivity to sunlight (76 percent) and to electrical and magnetic fields (54 percent). These individuals also reported electrical equipment such as TVs, computers, and light bulbs acting abnormally in their presence (20 to 24 percent). All of these phenomena are energy-related.

Atwater found 85 percent of the respondents claimed to have had an NDE, during which at least half of their experience was filled with bright, all-consuming etheric light. And 52 percent said they'd merged into and joined as one with this light or being of light.

Atwater describes her own life-changing experience:

> It is a million suns of compressed light dissolving everything
> unto itself, annihilating thought and cell, vaporizing human-
> ness and history, into the one great brilliance of all that is and
> all that ever was and all that ever will be. You know that it is
> God.

Atwater writes that the real power that emerges from near-death experiences is a collective one, the sum of the many: "When you have listened to the thousands I have, you take note…for the collective message that emerges speaks with a voice of thunder. "

In writing about her experiences, Atwater describes a step-up of energy at the moment of death, an increase in speed as if she were suddenly vibrating faster than before. She compares this acceleration of energy to having lived all of one's life at a certain radio frequency, when all of a sudden someone or something comes along and flips the dial: "That flip shifts you to another, higher wavelength. The original frequency…is still there…Only you changed, only you speeded up to allow entry into the next radio frequency on the dial."

You will recall that scientists believe that all possible events of the past, present, and future are "out there" in parallel universes. Atwater's analogy is amazingly close to the radio analogy Nobel Laureate Steven Weinberg and physicist Michio Kaku used to explain why people cannot detect parallel universes.

Atwater describes existence and reality. She uses television as an analogy, stating how the picture one sees is but a trick of perception. She says that what exists, what is really there, is quite literally one electron at a time fired from the back of the television:

> Your mind connects the electrons/dots into the picture images you think you see, while it totally ignores the true reality…Existence is a lot like television. What exists, what really exists, can't be fathomed by how it appears to operate or what it seems to be.

Atwater's analogy of the reality of television and electrons is surprisingly close to the realms of reality we discussed in Chapter 4. My speculation was based on scientific investigation. So, here again, we find both science and spirituality coming to the same conclusion.

Atwater also reports that near-death experiences change the physiology of the brain. She found that people who were right-brain dominated became left-brain dominated, and vice versa. Certainly, whether one is logical or intuitive, attentive to details or focused on big-picture issues, is somehow wired into the brain. What happens in NDEs that changes or alters the wiring? Certainly, opportunity for research exists in this interesting phenomenon.

SCIENTIFIC MEDICAL STUDIES OF NEAR-DEATH EXPERIENCES

As a scientist, I would put the preceding cases, although interesting, in the category of anecdotal. Here, "anecdotal" means an observation that might be true, but did not undergo and survive the process of a scientific publication, requiring peer review from anonymous referees accepting the validity of the findings.

Some scientific publications on near-death experiences have been "retrospective," meaning researchers planned or began the study after the NDE events. Although these studies provide scientific credence to this phenomenon, it might be argued that the interview subjects were selected in a biased fashion since the NDEs had already occurred. However, such studies show that, of adults and children who suffered life-threatening illnesses, 43 and 85 percent, respectively, had an NDE.

In 2001, a "prospective" study of near-death experiences was published by researchers headed by Pim van Lommel, a cardiologist, in the prestigious medical journal *The Lancet*. A prospective study plans the clinical trial before the events happen. This prospective study was designed to systematically investigate consecutive patients (thereby no selection), who survived cardiac arrest and who were verified as clinically dead.

The study involved 344 patients in 10 Dutch hospitals who had undergone 509 successful cardiopulmonary resuscitations (CPRs) between 1988 and 1992. The patients were interviewed as soon as physically possible, and also at two-year and eight-year intervals after the CPRs.

The results showed that 12 percent, or 41 patients, had a deep near-death experience, although 21 patients with superficial NDEs still had life-transformational changes. These levels were scored on the stages of NDEs reached: peace and well-being, body separation, entering the darkness, seeing the light, and entering the light.

Numerous life-changing behaviors and attitudes were statistically significant for those who had NDEs versus those who had no NDEs.

These transformations included a loss of their fear of death, a heightened belief in life after death, and a change to being more loving and empathic. Those who "died" but did not have NDEs, provided a control group, since they didn't experience these transformations.

These researchers stated that, "We did not show that psychological, neurophysiological, or physiological factors caused these [NDE] experiences." In other words, the NDEs were not the result of what physicians would consider normal psychological or physical phenomena. They noted that the NDEs were different from the experiences of people taking mind-altering drugs, receiving electrical stimulation to the temporal lobe (said to cause a phenomenon similar to an NDE), and other induced experiences. Van Lommel defined clinical death as: "a period of unconsciousness caused by insufficient blood supply to the brain because of inadequate blood circulation, breathing or both.

The cause of death in these studies was cardiac arrest; therefore, in addition to the definition above, the heart had stopped beating. During cardiac arrest the EEG becomes flat within 10 to 20 seconds from the onset of transient loss of consciousness.

The authors of this study wondered how, with flat EEGs (no measured brain function) during a period of clinical death (no breathing or heart activity), "clear consciousness outside one's body [could] be experienced." They further state that "NDE pushes at the limits of medical ideas about the range of human consciousness and mind-brain relation."

## WHAT OCCURS DURING AN NDE?

If the brain has shut down, how can one see a tunnel, or a light—or see or experience anything, for that matter? A possible explanation for NDEs is that when the brain shuts down, the person is still accessing the information realm—if mind and consciousness accesses this realm when the brain is quiet. Upon resuscitation, the brain retrieves the NDE memory by receiving upixels which contain the information.

Susan Blackmore, Senior Lecturer in psychology and a skeptic of spiritual explanations of NDEs, believes all NDEs can be explained by actions in the brain just before death or just after being revived. She disputes claims of NDEs occurring while the brain is inactive. Or, is she half right, the memory of the NDE is retrieved from the information realm via upixels after being revived? I decided to do additional investigating.

The M.D. Anderson Cancer Center in Houston, Texas is one of the largest and most prestigious cancer treatment facilities in the world. It was the first of many that I visited decades earlier in my quest to understand cancer and to find new healing agents. I returned to M.D. Anderson in October 2006. Ironically, my purpose this time was to understand death. Hundreds of physicians, nurses, hospice workers, educators, and members of the International Association of Near-Death Studies, who had experienced NDEs, participated in an international near-death conference.

Tall, slim Pim van Lommel with his eloquent Dutch accent encouraged further research on NDEs and out-of-body experiences, as well as on the theory and background of transcendence. Van Lommel believes NDEs occur while the brain is inactive.

London psychiatrist Peter Fenwick captivated the packed auditorium with his description of a planned NDE prospective clinical trial, which will attempt to resolve the question of whether NDEs occur during the absence of brain activity.

If scientific research can clearly show NDEs occur during a period of no concurrent brain activity, perhaps we will finally have scientific evidence of the spiritual. More prospective clinical trials on NDEs and consciousness are underway or being planned. Because of the number of participants needed to arrive at a statistically significant conclusion, it might take several years before such studies can resolve the relationship of NDEs to brain activities. Two anecdotal cases, however, are worthy of mention.

## A 200-MINUTE NDE

In his book *Light and Death*, cardiologist Michael Sabom relayed the experiences of a 35-year-old woman had an operation for a brain aneurysm in 1991. He called her "Pam Reynolds" in order to protect her identity.

At 7:15 a.m. Reynolds was brought into the operating room and given a general anesthetic, her eyes taped shut. Small molded speakers were inserted into her ears, emitting 11 to 33 clicks per second at 90 decibels—like a lawnmower blasting into her ears—to cause an EEG signal while brain activity was occurring. At 8:40 an artery in her groin was prepared for the cardiopulmonary bypass and her scalp was incised. At 10:50, the cooling of her blood and body began. By 11:00, her body temperature was 73 degrees Fahrenheit. Then cardiac arrest was induced. The EEG of her outer brain functioning went flat and brainstem functions weakened.

By 11:25 her body was at 60 degrees and the "clicks" from the ear speaker did not register any response from her EEG. She experienced total brain shutdown. The operating table was tilted up to drain the blood from her head. Her aneurysm was repaired and the procedures were reversed. At noon, her heart monitor indicated ventricular fibrillation. After two rounds of defibrillator shocks, her heart beat normally.

Reynolds recalls the sound of the drill. She can describe the drill, and she knew that the artery in her right groin was too small for a probe so the nurses had to use the left artery. Robert Spetzler, neurosurgeon and director of the Barrow Neurological Institute in Phoenix, cannot explain her recall since the instruments were covered while she was conscious, the artery discussion by the nurses occurred when she was under general anesthesia, and she had form-fitting speakers blasting lawnmower-level noise into her ears. "I do not have an explanation given the physiological state she was in," said Spetzler.

However, these recalled events occurred while there was still measurable brain activity as indicated by her EEG though her brain was certainly quiet compared to a normal waking state. Reynolds then described the rest of her NDE: moving through a tunnel, joyfully encountering several deceased relatives, experiencing light, and being told by her family members not to go farther into the light. Her deceased uncle led her back to her body, and she saw its terrible condition. She saw her body "jump" once, then, upon a second "jump," she felt her uncle push her back into it.

Most people receiving general anesthesia can recall nothing of the procedure even with a functioning brain at the time of the operation. With documented time sequences and definitive lack of brain activity during the later events of Reynolds' operation, which she remembered, her case is the strongest evidence for NDEs occurring during the absence of brain activity. Other anecdotal NDE cases suggest NDEs also occur during a flat EEG.

BLIND SIGHT

Blind at birth, Vicky Noratuk accurately "saw" herself and her wedding ring during an NDE, resulting in her first vision of what others see. In this case, the question of whether the NDE occurred while she was alive or "dead" is less important than the question of how she could have "seen" for the first time in her life during an NDE. Other cases of the blind having NDEs with similar experiences were also mentioned at the conference.

These cases and others where there was recall of events when the brain was inactive, or where there was sight in those who have never had sight, challenge Blackmore's and others' contention that all NDEs can be explained with the brain.

Then there is Stuart Hameroff, an anesthesiologist, who, along with physicist Sir Roger Penrose, postulates that quantum events in microtubules in the brain explain NDEs. Remember, one theory is that quantum events in the brain's microtubules lead to mind and consciousness. Hameroff believes that quantum entanglement of what I call upixels can create the NDEs after the brain is inactive "at least for a while."

## THE DEAD SPREADING THE NEWS

I have encountered numerous people who claim to have contact with the dead. Generally, they are afraid to tell their stories for fear of being regarded as delusional or worse. Yet, these individuals are adamant that their experiences occurred. They usually only tell people whom they trust. They rarely tell their doctor.

Bernie Siegel, a medical doctor who teaches the value of love in healing, has many stories of the dead or dying who communicate with loved ones:

> I have many letters from people who were…aware that an
> individual had died who was a great distance from them. A
> voice, a vision, a hand on the shoulder, and then the phone
> rang and they knew what the news would be.

Rupert Sheldrake, in his book *The Sense of Being Stared At*, devotes a chapter to this phenomenon of contacts with the dead or dying. In addition to his own research, he cites an earlier study in 1886, *Phantasms of the Living*, which reported 702 cases of the dying or dead communicating with a living person. Another study involved 410 data collectors and 17,000 interviewees in Britain. About 50 percent (85 people) had an experience of "contact" from the dead or dying. Calculations show that this phenomenon was 440 times more frequent than would be expected by chance.

Sheldrake notes that a commonality of such telepathy is a close emotional bond, such as those which exist between parents and children, identical twins, husbands and wives, lovers, and best friends. This suggests that the common ingredient is love. He also provides numerous examples of animals' abnormal behavior at the time of a human death, when the death was of someone close to the animal. Again, a love bond is the common thread.

Are the reported cases of near-death experiences and communication from the dead and dying sufficient evidence for the existence of an afterlife? No. The late Carl Sagan summed it up with his philosophy that extraordinary claims require extraordinary data.

Suppose that prospective NDE clinical trials offer more evidence of NDEs occurring while the brain is inactive. A critic might then concede that the information realm might be accessed, but then contend that this is only for the cases when the person comes back to life and not in the cases of actual death. So, how could anyone ever produce evidence of the dead being out there in the information realm, or anywhere else? This brings us to another 21st-century study which attempts to provide evidence that the dead are out there. Or, perhaps, still with us.

## HOW TO PROVE AN AFTERLIFE?

In 2002, Gary Schwartz's *The Afterlife Experiments* was published. In this work, Schwartz documents his attempts to scientifically address the seemingly intractable problem of producing experiments that would scientifically prove the existence of an afterlife. Schwartz, a Ph.D. graduate from Harvard, is a renowned psychologist with over 400 publications and a former tenured professor at Yale University. At the University of Arizona, he pursued interdisciplinary research.

How do you have conversations with the dead? A psychic often contacts a dead person through a living relative of the deceased, an individual known as a "sitter." Presumably, the sitter allows the psychic to access the dead. Studies documented in *The Afterlife Experiments* verified that certain psychics have the ability to access information about the dead relatives of sitters. The information, analyzed by using mathematical probabilities compared with random guesses, was amazingly specific. In one case, the accuracy of the psychic was 90 to 100 percent, including names and the correct spelling of names. In many cases, the message from the dead to the living was, "I am okay, and you will be okay, too."

Schwartz makes his experiments available for scrutiny by detailing them in his book, videotaping them, and publishing the results in scientific, peer-reviewed journals. He takes seriously all of the criticisms and suggestions for modifications of his experiments, which increase in sophistication as the study and experiments progress.

As a scientist and a born skeptic, I found myself attempting to poke holes in his experiments, conceiving alternative explanations, and (mentally) designing modified experiments...But alas, by the end of the book, all of my issues were addressed, and nearly all of them were satisfied. Schwartz describes his own skepticism, his discovery of deception in certain cases, and his ongoing education in the art of deception.

Schwartz's research supports the speculation that the body and brain are receivers and transmitters of electromagnetic energy, and the evidence he presents supports the belief in an afterlife. Does this evidence prove an afterlife, though? The evidence is intriguing, but it isn't enough to prove there is an afterlife. But then again, is it reasonable to demand proof? It is unreasonable to demand proof of the afterlife just as all of the modern scientific theories are by definition not proved and are, in fact, not provable. What is reasonable to expect is more evidence.

What may be concluded is that the afterlife experiments of Schwartz, when combined with the NDE phenomenon, offer intriguing hints of an afterlife.

### REINCARNATION: ANOTHER POPULAR BOOK SUBJECT

I have witnessed so-called "past-life" experiences during hypnosis sessions when I was a student of hypnotherapy. Once, under hypnosis, a young woman spoke of a city in Eastern Europe. No one, including the woman (after she came out of hypnosis), had ever heard of the place. Later, the instructor did some research and, indeed, the city existed.

The woman had regressed to a past life in the 1700s.

There are several potential explanations for this past-life experience. One is that the woman had such a past life. Another is that she somehow heard of the city and placed the knowledge in her subconscious, which was accessed during hypnosis. Or, perhaps she did not have a past life at all, and was accessing the information from the universe. Finally, she might have simply made it up, and luck had it that such a city existed in Eastern Europe at that time. The ability to speak a foreign language or the knowledge of an event in the past (later verified through extensive research) could be explained by so-called genetic memory, wherein memories from ancestors are somehow held in our cells.

Like with the near-death stories, there are numerous books about reincarnation and thousands of reported cases (some recalled by past-life experiences). Critics do not question the phenomena, but rather the explanation.

## IS IT IMPORTANT HOW YOU DIE?

In *The Tibetan Book of the Living and Dying,* our existence is divided into continuously linked events: life, dying, death, after-death, and re-birth, or becoming one with God. To the Tibetan Buddhist, the moment of death is important. Much of the Tibetan Buddhist monk's time is spent in preparation for death. They believe that the moment is filled with potential, and that it should not be feared. For these monks, death is but another chapter of life—and not the final chapter at that. If one flees from being one with God, he will miss his chance. One must cling to the part of the mind that survives and relinquish the part of the mind that dies.

Then, what survives? Sogyal Rinpoche, author of *The Tibetan Book of the Living and Dying,* writes that the Tibetan Buddhist believes that the mind survives. He likens dying to losing your passport; it does not mean that you cease to exit spiritually. His thesis may seem strange to Westerners: you lose your identity, but you are the same person. Charles Tart, a psychologist and the author of articles on the afterlife, agrees that it is unlikely that ordinary personality survives. Tart further suggests that altered states, resulting from meditation or mind-altering drugs, produce consciousness that might be similar to what survives death.

Colin Wilson, the British author, contends that the evidence for survival after death is as strong as the evidence for black holes. At the time of his statement (1990), this was perhaps true. Since then, however, black holes have become more accepted and are predicted to be at the center of most galaxies. It can be argued that we need an equal effort, similar to the numerous scientists looking for evidence of black holes, to investigate the afterlife.

## OPPOSING VIEWS

Many logical scientific explanations exist for people's accounts of near-death experiences. One of these is that the person did not die at all and the brain was still active, but instruments were either not used or were too insensitive to detect brain activity. In some cases, significant embellishment of the memory could explain the story. Some NDEs might even be "false memories," which the brain is known to be capable of providing. Combinations of any of these possibilities are also plausible. Blackmore's suggestion, that the NDE might result from brain activity an instant before "death" or an instant after being revived, might be valid for some cases.

However, some NDEs cannot be explained by any of these possibilities. In those cases, what is happening?

NDEs—accessing the information realm?

Can the 21st-century revelation of an information realm containing all past, present, and future events be consistent with spiritual essence, or the soul, or upixels? The energy fields described in Chapter 9 could be linked to this information realm.

Brinkley described his obsession to build an electrical device that would enable people to access the spiritual realm and predict future events. Atwater, in her survey of thousands of individuals who experienced near-death, wrote of their sensitivity to sunlight (which is electromagnetic energy) and to electrical and magnetic fields. She went on to describe the abnormal behavior of electrical devices when these individuals were present.

Like Brinkley, Atwater's subjects also exhibited ESP and an ability to predict the future. Of ESP, she wrote: "My experience has been that, although appearing as different abilities and manifestations, psychism is really just differing expressions of one mechanism—the extension of faculties normal to us."

### ARE WE RECEIVERS AND BROADCASTERS OF ENERGY?

All of these features might be explained by abnormal sensitivity to electromagnetic energy. Does this abnormal sensitivity occur when the brain goes into a certain state, such as that which could happen in near-death, meditation, prayer, or hypnosis? Did our ancestors possess this characteristic, and have we lost it due to lifestyles?

If our bodies and brains are receivers and transmitters of energy, these observations are explicable. The idea that the brain/body is a receiver is consistent with the observations of Valerie Hunt, who studied individuals sensitive to electromagnetic energy. Such energy produces emotions, consciousness, and thoughts. It is a fact that the energy we generate radiates through the universe; an ability to read others' thoughts could mean we are simply receiving others' transmissions. The upixels we generate through our bodies/brains may be projected into the universe for others to access via ESP.

Sheldrake states that the psyche "…is not confined to the body even during *life*…Telepathy is a natural, rather than a supernatural phenomenon." He points out many possible explanations for telepathy, including quantum processes in the brain, or an energy field surrounding all life. "…the recognition that our minds extend beyond our brains liberates us…We are interconnected."

Does it seem outlandish that humans, or any creature, can pick up energy emissions from another creature? Consider that sharks have recently been found to have hundreds of receptors connected to their brains which allow them to detect extremely weak electric fields generated by other animals. How weak? Neurobiologist and shark expert R. Douglas Fields at the National Institute of Health compares the one millionth of a volt detection capability of sharks being equivalent to "a voltage gradient created by a 1.5-volt AA battery with one pole dipped in the Long Island Sound and the other pole in waters off Jacksonville, Florida."

## HOW MUCH EVIDENCE IS NEEDED?

Do the reported cases of out-of-body, after-death, and near-death episodes, and contacts from the dead and dying, prove we survive death? No. They provide evidence for paranormal events as explained earlier by Tart. As he points out, what survives might not be what we think of as ourselves. But the upixels or information that we are made of is in our universe, at least for an instant, and they may have an existence somewhere in other dimensions or universes. Certainly the upixels and information survive our death. Humans are energy and, long after death, a person's energy will still abide. The upixels that make up all life will still exist after death. And the information will always be in the information realm, according to scientists.

All of the theories of science and all of the teachings of religions and spirituality are but metaphors that attempt to describe reality. There is agreement that we do not know what is really "out there."

## LOVE ENTANGLEMENT?

So what scientific metaphor might explain NDEs and communication with the dead? In quantum theory, when two or more particles (upixels) interact, they become "entangled," and an action on one can be observed instantly in another. As discussed in Chapter 4, this is also called nonlocality—or, as Einstein once remarked, "spooky action-at-a-distance." Hameroff proposes that entanglement can explain NDEs.

Could it be that the upixels which create us somehow become "entangled" with love? Most religions and spirituality have love as an essential element in their teachings. Stefan Einhorn, a professor of oncology and author of *A Concealed God*, summarizes such teachings:

> The major religions all claim that love of our fellow human
> beings also leads to a deeper understanding of the fact that we
> are all fundamentally part of the same divine context...This
> idea of love between God and humankind and between one
> human being and another is a theme and variations that is an
> inherent part of the fabric of the great religions.

Love is a proven factor in healing. It is interesting, too, that a love bond is a common factor in communication with the dead and dying. Love is found as a factor in numerous reports, including those from the NDE Dutch clinical experiments, as well as those from the studies made by Siegel, Sheldrake, and Schwartz. Atwater describes the involvement of love, the being of light, in her own near-death experience and in her survey of thousands of others NDEs.

Could it be that love is an essential aspect of the information or rules that transform the upixels into our reality?

METAPHORS THEN AND NOW

We have perceptual difficulties with more than three spatial dimensions and the concept of parallel universes. We have difficulty expressing the ultimate reality with equations, words, and theories. Still, science has been valuable in nearly every area of our modern lives. We have learned how to heal the body and understand ourselves and our place in the universe. We have progressed from myth and metaphor to science via religion and spiritual teachings, and back again to metaphor.

Author Gary Doore reminds us of William James, who taught that in order to establish a friendship with another person, we must trust the person beyond any evidence at hand. Doore states that, in like manner, we must trust the universe that our spirit's virtue and wisdom will continue to grow after death.

Schwartz, who found evidence of consciousness in the afterlife, poses the question: Suppose the human spirit lives forever? Suppose it is proven. How would our lives be affected? I believe the answer is a spiritual awakening in which we heal our spirits.

> *I believe there is no source of deception in the investigation of nature which can compare with a fixed belief that certain kinds of phenomena are impossible.*

> –William James

> *I think spirituality is part of healing…I thnk death is not just an end but perhaps a beginning as well. From my experience I feel that we do live on in some other form of energy after the body dies. I don't say this to make people feel better, but because I have seen and heard about such extraordinary even*

> –Bernard (Bernie) S. Siegel

# 11
# HEALING THE RIFT

*There is no difficulty that enough love will not conquer, no dis-*
*ease that enough love will not heal, no door that enough love*
*will not open, no gulf that enough love will not bridge, no wall*
*that enough love will not throw down, no sin that enough love*
*will not redeem... A sufficient realization of love will dissolve*
*it all. If only you could love enough you would be the happiest*
*and most powerful person in the world...*

–Emmet Fox

As is the case with most of us, the simple world of my youth began like a trickle from melting snow and merged into the stream of life's complexities. Dreams provided me buoyancy, purpose, and hunger, illuminating a path that left only hazy memories in my wake.

By adolescence my tears and the tears of all those around me transformed the stream into a river. I chased my personal rainbow, ignoring the injuries from the rapids and the waterfalls. I never looked back.

I became consumed by the complex world of conflicting dogmas as I meandered by tide pools of riddles and mysteries. I sought wisdom as a guide in my quest to reach the sea. What I ultimately found was unfathomable.

It is a bottomless ocean extending infinitely in all directions. We and our world are but one wave on the surface of this ocean. We are lost in the multitude of all the other waves. Our wave will not exist forever, but will merge with others and cease to exist. Beneath us and around us lie other worlds.

Humans have focused on the wave. They wonder: What was the origin of the wave? What is the wave? What happens when the wave ceases to exist?

We are familiar with physical waves in our world. Humans call the stuff of the wave, water. Yet the wave is created by all of the water in the ocean, for different water molecules are continually moving in and out of our wave. But this is too simplistic, for the water is made up of upixels that are zipping in and out of this world trillions of times a second.

The wave did not begin with the creation of water; it began with the creation of the upixels. However, no one knows when, how, or why the upixels were created. The upixels are energy, so the wave is an illusion. It is immaterial energy. The ocean is an illusion for it also is merely upixels, energy. There is so much we do not know about this world. We don't know where the upixels go when they disappear. We don't know where the new upixels come from when they zip into our world for an instant.

We can neither fathom an infinitely deep and extensive ocean, nor comprehend the meaning of other dimensions or worlds. We perceive only a trillionth of what our world is, so we focus on the wave that is within our perceptive capacity. We have splintered into factions, each faction believing that they understand the wave, know what caused the formation of the wave, and comprehend what happens when the wave ceases to exist.

But the ancient sages and spiritual leaders teach us that all of this is truly beyond our comprehension. They speak of the essence of the wave surviving forever, long after it disappears. They agree that, somehow, energy creates our reality. They agree that we are one with nature and everything in the universe. They agree that our immaterial essence survives death.

Where did we come from? No one knows. The creation of our universe and the origin of life remain—and may always remain—a mystery. But current scientific concepts are able to describe the unique aspects of our world and the gift of life. Science is likely to gain additional understanding of our universe and life's origins, but the complete answer is likely to be elusive for a very long time.

Science, for at least two millennia, has added its knowledge to the spiritual knowledge. Upixels pass through us a billion, trillion, trillion, trillion times a second and exit to other universes. Somehow, they create space, energy, existence, and reality itself. Like the electrons used to light up the pixels on a computer or television screen, the upixels of the universe carry energy and information that create our consciousness and reality.

But we access only a small fraction of the upixels of this unfathomably expansive universe. In accessing the upixels, we are merely tapping into the information they possess. What information is available from the upixels we cannot access? Some individuals are able to access an additional small fraction of the upixels, and experience what we call "paranormal" events of extrasensory perception, "psychic" ability, precognition, spiritual healing, placebo effects, the power of prayer, and an entire world of spiritual experience.

Where are we going? We are energy waves, buzzing through the universe at a speed of over a million miles per hour. Our energy merges with everything in the universe, and we are all connected. We are all created from upixels, and each and every upixel is connected and instantly senses the action on other upixels. We are going everywhere and nowhere. Like the water making up a wave, we came from the ocean and we will return to the ocean.

## WHAT WILL WE BECOME?

Our energy merges with the energy and space of the universe. Our upixels will recycle into everything that exists and ever will exist.

Time is an illusion. It is a measurement that is purely a human construct, created to lend a sense of order and direction to the energy "out there." Each moment of our existence is like a video-recorded event, stored somewhere in the universe. But life's immaterial essence, the spirit, will survive and live on for eternity. Thus, life's immaterial essence survives death. There are many metaphors to choose from as to what life's upixels become. They might be zipping through other dimensions or universes where people live on, or are reincarnated, or live in heavenly bliss.

We can affect our future. When we act with love and compassion, with a common mind for a common good, we can set the course of our future. One of the greatest contributions of spirituality would be an awakening that is truly planetary, that unites and ignites our power of free will, leading to transcendence.

## HEALING THE RIFT

The rift between science and spirituality disappears when modern concepts of science are compared to ancient spiritual wisdom. In other words, spirituality can illuminate 21st-century science by providing meaning and answering the question, "Why?"

Science will continue to inch toward a better understanding of the creation of our universe and life. It will go on to improve our lifestyles and our health. Science will also keep searching for the truth about "what" and "how," and it is my hope that this search will be enhanced by spiritual understanding.

Like the other creatures with whom we share the Earth, humans have a limited capacity to understand and perceive what is "out there," and nearly all of the picture is missing. Science and spirituality, therefore, share the resulting sense of humility and awe of the mystery of it all.

Science continually modifies its teachings and hunts obsessively for more information in an effort to arrive at the truth. Spirituality accepts that most of the important aspects of our world are missing and that they are impossible to comprehend. It names the missing pieces God, spirit, and soul. By sharing their teachings, science and spirituality can continue to enlighten each other. In a sense, science and spirituality are complimentary—like yin and yang.

## THE ULTIMATE HEALING: THE UPIXELS AND LOVE

After a rigorous and lengthy search, I have come to understand that our existence is the ultimate mystery as seen by science, and as understood through spirituality. In my journey, I found that beyond upixels and energy, there is love and compassion. What greater clues do we need than the dead attempting to tell loved ones that they are okay, and that those who still live will be okay, too? With love and self-love, we can heal ourselves and others. But love is not restricted to healing bodies and minds. Love can heal the spirit. It is the ultimate healing.

The 20th century began with horse-drawn buggies and many social and class injustices. We ended it with rockets, airplanes, and much of the population of the first-world countries affluent and pursuing materialistic goals. But there is an undercurrent, a hunger for spirituality that can serve as our guide. Each of us needs to find grounding—a spiritual awakening that collectively will set a new course for mankind.

If the universe is mere information, the message it contains is love and compassion. Perhaps the rules of the universe have each upixel responding to compassion and love—or, perhaps, every upixel *is* compassion and love.

My journey was a quest to understand the fate of those who die. I discovered a universe consisting of a potpourri of mysteries, enigmas, and wonders. This is the world of the first act of our drama. The miracle of life includes a kaleidoscope of sights to deceive our perceptions of reality, a symphony of sounds to drum up memories, an array of delectable tastes to remind us of gratitude, an offering of subtle scents to appreciate nature, and a succession of intricate feelings to tempt us into believing that we are separate.

But all of this is an illusion—our bodies are the costumes in which we play our roles in life. Love is the only enduring truth, and death is not the final curtain. The next act reveals the real universe and the other 96 percent of its stage. The infinite stage that creates our world, the omnipotent force that powers our journey, and the epic script that we write—all these are proof of the wholeness we call love. All there is, and all that we truly need, is love.

# Notes

## Preface

P. i Carl Sagan quotation, see Sagan (1974) p. 287. Sagan was a twentieth century astronomer and author of Cosmos, the best-selling science book of all time.

P. vi Quotation by Einstein, see Targ (1998) p. 1.

## Chapter 1

P. 1 Episcopal priest Matthew Fox quote, see Miller (1992) p.53.

P. 1 For details on 10 West at UCLA, see Lax (1984).

PP. 3-4 For a discussion of what makes up what I call upixels and the universe see comments by Hooft (2005).

P. 5 Einstein and a static universe, see Ferguson (2004) p. 75, Kaku (2005) p. 37.

P. 6 For the complexities of distance from the expansion since the Big Bang, see Lineweaver (2005). For complexities of distance in the universe, see Bartusiak (2004).

P. 6 Inflation, for a discussion of the timing, see Seife (2003) p. 63-68. No one knows the size of the universe at this instant in time or the exact degree of expansion. One speculation is that it might have expanded from $10^{21}$ times smaller than an atom to the size of a cantaloupe. The example used in the text uses a conservative estimate of an expansion of about $10^{27}$. Those scientists who believe in the concept of inflation do not agree on the size of the universe at the time of expansion or the size at the end of expansion.

P. 6 Scientific Notation-abbreviation of large and small numbers. Scientific notation needs to be explained. For numbers greater than of plus 10, scientists use the "shorthand" of 10 to some power. For example, rather that saying 100,000 they use $10^5$. Rather than a 16 trillion, scientist use

1.6 X $10^{13}$. The superscript denotes the number of zeros to add starting at the decimal point, therefore 1.6 with 13 zeros is 16,000,000,000,000. For numbers less than one a minus sign is placed before the superscript. Rather than saying, 0.000005, scientist use 5 X $10^{-6}$. Notice we moved the decimal six places to the right hence $10^{-6}$.

P. 7 Particle accelerators and the temperatures created by them versus the Big Bang, see Riordan and Zajc (2006).

P. 7 Higgs field, see Greene (2004) pp. 258-271.

P. 8 Microwave background, see Greene (2004) p. 515.

P. 8 Problems with the Big Bang theory, see Moring (2002) pp. 225-236.

P. 8 Parallel universes, see Tegmak (2004 and 2005). See Deutsch (1997), Rees (1997), and Kaku (2005) pp. 92-3.

PP. 8-9 Penrose (2004) pp. 757-778. Penrose admits that he is a skeptic of the inflation theory.

P. 9 Comments about Rees, see Kaku (2005) pp. 249-255.

P. 10 Quotation from Penrose, see Penrose (2004) pp. 764-5.

P. 10 First stars, see Larson (2004) and Miralda-Escude (2003). Although some have speculated on massive early stars of 1,000 times the mass of our sun, recent results question whether stars can exist that are more that about 150 times the mass of our sun, see Figer (2005).

P. 10 Supernovae, see Gehrels (2004).

PP. 10-1 Chemicals created in stars, see Kwok (2004), Sneden (2003) and Eid (2005). P. 11 Eddington quote, see Webster (2005) p. 298.

P. 11 Mystery of dark energy and dark matter, see Seife in Science (2003), Irion (2003), Rowan (2003), Ostriker (2001 and 2003), Krauss (2004), Dvali (2004 and 2004), Kirshner (2003) and Hooper (2006).

P. 12 Michael Turner and the absurd universe, see Seife (2003) p. 90.

P. 12 Dark matter responsible for the speed of star and galaxy formation, see Kanipe (2006) p. 86.

P. 13 Dark energy "the biggest question in physics," see Seife (Science 2003).

P. 13 Formation of our solar system, see Kenyon (2004), Valley (2005) and Kerr (2004).

P. 14 Mars size object created the moon, see Tyson (2004) pp. 191-2. For age of moon, see Lee (1997).

PP. 14-15 Mass increase due to numerous impacts, see Oro (2002) p. 31. Comets come from two sources: the Oort cloud containing millions of comets, but this source is the most distant and only when some perturbation occurs like a passing star will one or more be dislodged and head for our inner solar system The other source from the Kuiper belt (just beyond planet Neptune) produces comets of greater regularity.

P. 16 Tyson's quotation on origins, see Tyson (2004) p. 183.

P. 16 Polkinghorne's quotation, see Kaku (2005) p. 248.

P. 17 John Wheeler's suggestion that consciousness is needed for reality, see Gardner (2007) p. 184.

P. 17 Sagan's quotation, see Sagan (1980) p. 4.

## Chapter 2

P. 18 Gale quotation, see Gale and Hauser (1988) p. 32. Gale is a M.D., Ph.D. immunologist and oncology expert. He helped in the aftermath of the Chernobyl nuclear accident.

P. 21 Hoyle on probability of life, see Fry (2000) p. 196.

P. 22 Definition of life from Crick, see Crick (1981) p. 56; for a more detailed description and discussion of life, see Gleiser (2004) pp. 642-645 and pp. 650-652 and Kauffman (2004).

P. 23 What complex molecules are essential for life? Chemistry of life, see Dobson (2004).

P. 24 RNA Knoll (2003) p. 80. Knoll also describes the difficulties in interpreting fossils for signs of microbial life since the evidence is so subtle.

For discussions on RNA and early life, see Ferris (1998), James (1998) and Orgel (1986). Modified RNA, see Fry (2000) pp. 242-9.

P. 24 Quotation from Orgel, see Orgel (2002) p. 154.

P. 25 Cronin quotation, see Cronin (1998) p. 140.

PP. 25-26 For production of complex organic compounds from simple ingredients, see Kim (1978 and 1978) and Wald (1978, 1978).

P. 26 Micrometeorites and Maurette quote, see Maurette (1998).

P. 27 Microbes deep in the Earth, see Lane (2005). p. 22.

P. 28 Titan, Griffith (2006).

P. 28 Did life come from space? See Fry (2000) p. 201.

PP. 28-29 Life on Mars, see Brack (1998), Klein (1996), Nealson (1997), McKay (1996, 1998) and Soloman (2005). Recent new evidence of life on Mars, see Fisk (2006).

P. 29 Hoyle discussion, see Hoyle (1979 and 1979).

P. 30 Conditions for life, see Tyson (2004) p. 251.

P. 30 Quotation from Schoff, see Schoff (2002) p. 6.

P. 31 Quotation from Fry, see Fry (2000) p. 283.

P. 32 Protons pumped across membranes, see Lane (2005) pp. 85-104.

P. 33 Black Elk quotation, see Miller (1992) p. 83. Also known as Nicholas Black Elk, he was a spiritual authority who witnessed the Battle of Little Bighorn in 1876.

## Chapter 3

P. 34 Quotation from Russell, see Webster (2005) p. 705. Russell was a twentieth-century British philosopher, mathematician, essayist and social critic.

P. 35 Humans are a composite of many species, see Baeckhed (2005).

PP. 37-39 First life on earth, see Moorbath (2005). First photosynthesis, see Beukes (2004) and Tice (2004). Oxygen, build-up of oxygen in earth's atmosphere, see Knoll (2003) pp. 157-60, pp 218-9, and pp. 222-4 and Schoff (1998) pp 352-3. Methane producing organism 3.5 million years ago, see Canfield (2006) and Ueno (2006); additional evidence for life 3.5 million years ago, see Allwood (2006).

PP. 38-40 Communal evolution, see Dyson (2005); for a somewhat contrary opinion in which natural selection started with molecular replication, see de Duve (2005).

P. 40 Formation of multicellular organism, see Bloom (2000) pp. 27-28 and Margulis (1986). Modern amoeba clustering, see Brand and Yancey (1980) p. 25.

P. 40 Clams, see Bloom (2000) pp. 26-7 and pp. 29-30.

P. 41 The earth's explosion of new organisms, for a detailed discussion of the impact of eyes on evolution, see Parker (2003). The author speculates that oxygen may have played an important role in the evolution of eyes since significant oxygen levels permeated the oceans about 580 millions years ago as reported by Kerr ((2006).

P. 41 Missing link–fish to land animals, see Ahlberg (2006), Daeschler (2006) and Shubin (2006).

PP. 41-42 Mass extinctions of 251 million years ago, see Benton (2004) and Lane (2007).

P. 42 Dinosaurs, for details on fossils found in the Burgess Shale, see Briggs (1994).

PP. 42-43 From ape to man, apes are believed to be about 20 million years old, but we are discussing the more recent evolution of the apes to yield man.

P. 43 Humans using language memes, see Bloom (2000) pp. 62-3. For suggested timing of humans using language about 40,000 years ago, see Dowling (2004) pp. 58-62.For a brief summary of the evolution of man, see Mithen (1996) pp. 17-32, some of the data for Table 3 was obtained from this source. For a discussion of some of the controversies concerning timing of events of early humans, see Wong (2005).

PP. 44-45 An example of bacterial evolution: Bacillus thuringensis is bacteria having an insecticidal protein. For discussions of its diversity and implied evolution see Feitelson (1992) and (1993) pp. 63-71, and Kim (1993). Although the term "co-evolution" is used here, scientists holding to a strict definition of the term would object. The author means to convey the concept of a species of bacteria evolving and taking advantage of a mutation in the toxin for its survival.

P. 45 The mechanisms for evolution: DNA shuffling, rearrangements and mutations;for general discussion on mutations see Lewin pp. 699-702.

P. 47 Microbes resistant to radioactivity, D. radiodurans, nicknamed, "Conan the bacterium," see Krasner (2002) p. 41.

P. 47 Unidentified organisms in mouth and gut, see Pennisi (2005) and Baeckhed (2005).

P. 48 Camouflage of octopuses, see Hanlon (1999).

P. 49 Digital organisms, see Zimmer (2005) and www.dllab.caltech.edu/avida

P. 51 Darwin quote, see Kaplan (2001) p. 3.

## Chapter 4

P. 55 Henry's quotation, see Henry (2005).

P. 56 Einstein's greatest blunder, see Kaku (2005) p. 51.

P. 56 Dark energy as a percent of the universe, see Nadis (2004) pp. 100-105 and Livio (2004).

P. 57 Particles created in space, see Laughlin (2005) pp. 102-3 and Al-Khalili (2003) pp. 170-5.

P. 57 Laughlin's quotation on the vacuum or space, see Laughlin (2005) p. 17. For space like a piece of glass and Einstein's rejection of the ether, see Laughlin (2005) p. 121; similarities of empty space and low temperatures, see Laughlin (2005) p. 105.

P. 58 Wilczek, see Wilczek (2006) p. 24.

PP. 58-59 Rees' factors for life, see Kaku (2005) pp. 249-53.

P. 60 String theory, see Brumfiel (2005), Witten (2004) and Schilling (2005).

P. 60 Guth and Kaiser, vacuum states and the number of possible vacuum states, see Guth (2005) and references therein.

P. 62 Why Planck's distance of $10^{-35}$ meters, see Smolin (2001) p. 169-170.

P. 62 Concept of electrons popping in and out of existence, being in parallel universes, needing these features to hold molecules together and Kaku quote, see Kaku (2005) pp.146-180.

P. 62 Satinover's quotation on Feynman and Wheeler, see Satinover (2001) p. 214.

P. 63 Bohr quotation, see Kaplan (2001) p. 222.

P. 63 Feynman's quotation, see Feynman (1963) p. 37-41 and Kaplan (2001) p. 131.For other examples used by famous physicists in reducing the question to quantum terms, see Webb (2004) pp. 3-4.

PP. 63-64 Particle or wave? See Feynman (1963) Vol. I, section 37 and Vol. III, sections 1 and 2, and Zeilinger (2004) pp. 202-9.

P. 64 Steven Hawking quotation, see Lewin (2005) p. 3.

P. 65 Nonlocality, see Greene (2004) pp.80-4, 114-5, 120-3 and Moring (2002) pp. 269-71. Entanglement, see Ball (2004).

PP. 65-66 The reason the slot machines can not be exposed to other slots in this fictitious example is that entanglement with the other slot machines will ruin the effect. Thus, in experiments with photons or other upixels, great care must be taken not to expose the upixels to others.

P. 67 Bohm's quotation, see Friedman (1990) pp. 89-90.

P. 68 Quotation of Tenzin Gyatso, His Holiness the Dali Lama, see Gyatso (2005) pp. 46-7.

P. 69 Eddington quotation, see Halpern and Wesson (2006) p. 215.

P. 69 The universe is but information, see Lloyd and Ng (2004), Lloyd (2006) and Wolfram (2002).

P. 70 Plato's Allegory of the Cave and the hypothetical physicist ponderings, see Webb (2004) pp. 4-7.

P. 70-73 Realms of reality. There are speculations and hypotheses that the other dimensions and universes might be at a larger size than $10^{-35}$ meters; for a discussion on these points, see Webb (2004) pp. 245-277. For a discussion of Planck's time, see Greene (2004) pp. 350-1, pp. 333-4 and pp. 473-4.

P. 74 Douglas Adams quotation, see Kaplan (2001) p. 207.

P. 75 Wofgang Pauli quotation was a letter to M. Fierz, August 12, 1948, see Schwartz and Begley (2002) opening page. Pauli was a twentieth-century physicist who made several major contributions including understanding atomic structure and quantum theory.

## Chapter 5

P. 76 Haldane quote, see http://whatthebleep.com/quotes. John Burdon Sanderson Haldane was a twentieth-century British geneticist and evolutionary biologist.

P. 78 The upside down experiment described by Tiller, see Tiller (1997) pp. 149-150.

P. 79 We evolved to see false images. See Talbot (1991) pp. 162-4, Crick (1994) pp.26-57 and Bloom (2000) pp. 66-7.

P. 79 Eddington, see Witham (2005) p. 123.

P. 80 False color, see Land (1957, 1977) and Sacks (1997). Also see under Google search color vision and click on www.glenbrook.k12.il.us/gbss-ci/phys/Class/light/u1212b.html or see The Island of the Colorblind; see Sacks (1997) for an Anthropologist on Mars; see Sacks (1995), see the chapter on "the case of the colorblind painter." Sack's quotation, see Sacks (1995) p. 41. For a more technical discussion on color, see Feynman (1963) Vol. 1 pp 35-2 to 35-10.

P. 80 Multimind, see Ornstein (1986) p. 40.

PP. 81-82 Wilczek (2006) pp. 72-80.

P. 82 The perception of time, see Fritzsch (1996), Rees (1997) pp. 116-8 and Gott (2001).

PP. 82-83 Oldest fossils, see Kanipe (2006) p. 52.

P. 83 Einstein's quotation and discussion of time, see Greene (2004) p. 139.

P. 84 Parallel universes' strangeness, see Seife (2004).

P. 84 Weinberg's analogy and Kaku's quotation, see Kaku (2005) p. 170.

P. 85 Laughlin quote, see Laughlin (2005) pp. 209-211.

PP. 85-86 Time, physicist Julian Barbour, like Greene, contends there is no such thing as time or motion and that our perceptions of reality would be totally different with such a paradigm, see Barbour (1999).

P. 86 Fifth dimension of space, see Halpern and Wesson (2006) p. 211.

P. 86 Time and entanglement, Clegg (2006) p. 127.

P. 86 Vedral quotation, see Vedral (2003).

P. 86 Penrose, see Clegg (2006) p. 240.

P. 86 Josephson quotation, see Clegg (2006) p. 226.

P. 91 Einstein quotation, see Kaplan (2001) p. 8.

# Chapter 6

P. 96 Ornstein quotation, see Ornstein (1993) pp. 187-8.

P. 96 Many procedures exist for extracting DNA, check Google—key words: DNA isolation, also see: http://gslc.genetics.utah.edu/units/activities/extraction/.

P. 97 The development of the embryo, see Leroi (2003). For days 7, 13, 14, see Leroi (2003) pp. 35-6. Brain twisting at week 34, see Ornstein (1997) p. 149. Neurological development at 6 months, see Noble (2003) p. 101. Production of neurons in first 4 months, at birth and formation of brain at 60 days, see Dowling (2004) pp. 7-14.

P. 98 The human genetic code—the landmark publication of the taking the earlier draft of the human genome and creating a highly accurate sequence of the human genome, see International Human Genome Sequencing Consortium (2004), in this article the authors calculated that humans have between 20,000 and 25,000 protein coding genes.

PP. 98-99 Networks and biological networks—general references to networks and network theory, see Buchanan (2002), Watts (2003) and Jasny (2003). For references to biological networks, see Bray (2003) and Alon (2003). For discussions of how genes and networks influence behavior in various organisms, see Ridley (2004), Pennisi (2005) and Spiney (2005).

P. 99 See Pert (1999 and 2002).

PP. 100-1 See Becker (1985 and 1990). Quotation, Becker (1985) p. 21.

P. 101 Brain networks—how a cascade of chemical reactions produce memories, see Fields (2005).

P. 101 Quotation from Hamer and configurations of the brain, see Hamer (2004) pp. 96-7.

P. 103 Einstein's brain missing a fold, see Ackermann (2004) pp. 63-5.

PP. 103-4 Ornstein reference to high and low gain people, see Ornstein (1993) pp. 51-59.

P. 104 Humans born with only 25% of adult brain and visual system and Ornstein quote, see Ornstein (1993) pp. 10-12.

P. 105 Age versus brain development, see Dowling (2004) pp. 7-14.

P. 106 Babies, music and Zatorre quote, see Zatorre (2005).

P. 107 Age versus critical activities in children, for general discussion of early experience and the fine tuning of synaptic connections, see Kandel (1991) pp. 945-58. For an excellent review of current concepts of the development of a child's brain/mind, see Mithen (1996) pp. 33-60.

P. 108 In table, comments about the number of words in the vocabulary of a child and chimpanzee, see Dowling (2004) p. 59; accent after age 6, see p.

63; 869 sounds or phonemes, see p. 64.

PP. 109-10 Taste aversion, see Ornstein (1991) p. 69-70.

P. 111 Albert Szent-Gyorgyi quote, see Becker (1990) p. 116. Szent-Gyorgyi was a Hungarian medicinal chemist and the 1937 Noble Prize winner in medicine, honored for his work in vitamin C.

## Chapter 7

P. 112 Maharishi Mahesh Yogi quotation, see www.whatthebleep.com/quotes. He was the founder of transcendental meditation.

P. 115 The mind-matter theories, see Schwartz and Begley (2002) pp. 38-53.

PP. 116-17 Schwartz and Begley's comments on process philosophy, see Schwartz and Begley (2002) p. 45.

P. 117 Consciousness, see Searle (2004).

P. 119 For a discussion and interpretation of Leibniz's Monadology, see Rescher (1991) and Savile (2000).

P. 119 Stewart quotation of Leibniz, see Stewart (2006) p. 79. Stewart also describes the complex personality and motives of Leibniz in his book.

P. 122 OCD and Jeffrey Schwartz, see Schwartz and Begley (2002) pp. 54-95.

P. 122 Restak quotation, see Restak (2003) p.7.

PP. 122-23 Brain plasticity, for numerous examples including the blind seeing, stroke victims regaining motor control, pain control and many other examples, see Doidge (2007).

P. 123 Schwartz and Stapp quotation, see Schwartz and Begley (2002) p. 363.

P. 124 Smart wires, see Satinover (2001) p. 170 and pp. 230-7.

PP. 124-25 Microtubules for cell division of microbes (a common yeast), see Tanaka (2005). Microtubules in living organisms, see Satinover p. 156, pp. 162-3 and pp. 165-72. For general information on related molecules to microtubules in life forms, see Bray (2001) and for details on microtubules, see Bray (2001) pp. 171-89.

P. 126 Quantum mind: author and professor of cognitive sciences, Douglas Hofstadter (see Hofstadter 2007), explains consciousness and the concept of "I" with numerous strange loops created in the brain by computer-like processes (the specifics are not known and possibly well beyond human comprehension). Hofstadter contends (pp. 291-2) that the sense of "I" or consciousness is "a tremendously effective illusion" caused by strange loops and the source of these strange loops is perception. All of this is consistent with the hypothesis I present—perceptions are the receiving of information or upixels which (to use Hofstadter's metaphor) creates these strange loops (I describe them as complex intertwined webs of networks involving chemical and electrochemical processes). I agree with Hofstadter that all this results in the "illusion" that the brain creates consciousness and the sense of "I."

P. 126 Dyson's quote, see Dossey (1989) pp. 153-4.

P. 126 Wigner's quotation, see Schwartz and Begley (2002) p. 283.

P. 127 Eddington quote, see Halpern and Wesson (2006) p. 217.

P. 128 Sir James Hopwood Jeans, physicist, mathematician and astrophysicist quotation, see Carter (2002) p. 277.

## Chapter 8

P. 129 Rossi quotation see Rossi (1986) p. xiv.

P. 131 Erickson healing of patient, see Erickson (1980) Vol. II, pp. 182-3.

P. 133 Becker quotation and explanation of pain control, see Becker (1985) p. 239.

PP. 134-5 Quotation from Skeptics Dictionary and quotation from Margaret Talbot obtained from a Google search http://skepdic.com/placebo.html

P. 135 Tauber quote, see Tauber (2002).

P. 135 Since 1948 one million clinical trials, see Filmore (2004).

P. 136 Nocebo effect, see Noble (2003) pp. 129-133, 393, Barsky (2002), Hamer (2004) pp. 155-7 and Talbot (1991) pp. 90-2.

P. 136 Memories during anesthesia, see Chopra (1989) p. 163 and Dubovsky (1997) p. 259.

P. 137 Chopra's quote, see Chopra (1989) pp. 180-1.

P. 137-38 Number of people experiencing transcendental experiences and Carter's quote, see Carter (2002) pp. 278-9.

PP. 138-39 Newberg's quote, see Newberg (2001) p. 9. Brain location during prayer and meditation, see Newberg (2001) pp. 4-7.

P. 139 Prefrontal cortex thickening, see Lazar (2005).

P. 140 Gallup quote, see Tolson and Koenig (2003) p. 13.

P. 140 Dossey, data on controlled laboratory studies of prayer, see Dossey (1996) p. 49 and p. 219.

P. 141 Group meditation, see Dossey (1996) p. 144.

P. 141 Group prayer and Dr. Gardner, see Radin (1997) pp. 30-1.

P. 141 For a discussion on inconclusive results from group prayer, Radin (1997) pp. 150-1.

P. 142 Bernie Siegel, see Siegel (1986) and Siegel (1989) p. 3.

P. 142 Love and heart disease, see Ornish (1998).

P. 143 Straus and Straus (2006) p. 22.

P. 145 Jung's quote, see Miller (1992) p. 47.

P. 145 Author Saroyan's quote, see Siegel (1989) p. 227.

## Chapter 9

P. 149 Gregory of Nyssa quotation, see Einhorn (2002) front quotation page. He was a fourth-century bishop and saint who developed the doctrine of the Trinity and taught that God is infinite and therefore cannot be comprehended.

P. 151 Campbell (1990) p. 1.

P. 151 Einstein quotation, see Kaplan (2001) p. 181.

P. 152 Fox quotation, see Fox and Sheldrake (1996) pp. 85-6.

P. 153 Pearsall quote, see Schwartz and Russek (1999) p. xi-xii.

P. 154 Hunt, see Hunt (1996).

P. 156 Bone healing, see Becker (1985) p. 119, pp. 121-5, pp. 138-9, p. 149, p. 157, p. 163, pp. 170-2, pp.175-6, p. 179, p. 296.

P. 156 Wound healing using electric fields, see Zhao (2006).

P. 157 Tiller references to energy emissions, see Tiller (1997) pp. 134-8.

PP. 157-58 External energy (a magnetic field) affecting human behavior, see Doidge (2007) pp. 196-7

PP. 159-60 James Jeans quotation, see Dossey (1989) p. 121.

P. 160 Henry quotation, see Henry (2005).

P. 161 Targ and Katra quotation, see Targ and Katra (1998) pp. 18-9.

P. 163 Heisenberg quotation, see Witham (2005) pp. 133-4.

P. 163 Ward quotation, see Witham (2005) p. 141.

P. 164 Dyson and Blake quotes, see Kaplan (2001) pp. 226-7. Blake quote, see Kaplan (2001) p. 222. He was a twentieth-century physicist and mathematician famous for his work in quantum theory.

## Chapter 10

P. 165 Spinoza quote, see Webster (2001) p. 811. He was a seventeenth-century philosopher who wrote that God is not the transcendent creator of the universe but the infinity of nature describes God, in other words, the universe is a unitary whole.

P. 166 Discussion of afterlife beliefs in the West, see Segal (2004).

P. 168 The first death of Brinkley, see Brinkley (1994) pp. 4-53.

P. 169 Gallup poll of after death experiences see, Gallup (1982) p. 3, p. 6.

P. 169 Quotation from Brinkley, see Brinkley (1994) p. 127.

P. 170 Three death experiences, see Atwater (1994) pp. 132, 140, 142, 160-1, 174, 181-5, 194-7.

P. 172 Retrospective NDE studies, see van Lommel (2001).

P. 172 Dutch prospective clinical trials of NDEs, see van Lommel (2001).

PP. 173-74 What occurs during an NDE? General discussion of NDEs, see The Day I Died, a video by the British Broadcasting Company (BBC) in 2002.

P. 174 Susan Blackmore, see Blackmore (1991).

P. 174 Peter Fenwick, see Fenwick (1995) and Near-Death Experiences: 30 Years of Research—Implications for Health Care Professionals and Others Interested in the Phenomenon, October 25-8, 2006, at the University of Texas, M. D. Anderson Cancer Center, Houston, Texas.

P. 175 Robert Spetzler quotation, see Sabom (2003).

PP. 175-76 Pam Reynolds, see Sabom (1998); also the timing of events were presented and discussed at the Near-Death Experiences conference in Houston (see above reference).

P. 176 Vicky Noratuk, see The Day I Died, a video by BBC, 2002 and www.coasttocoastam.com/shows/2004/09/19.html.

P. 177 Stuart Hameroff, see Hameroff, Chalmers, and Kaszniak (1999). Hameroff quote in the video, The Day I Died.

P. 177 Siegel quote, Seigel (1989) p. 254.

P. 177 See Sheldrake (2003) pp. 68-82.

PP. 178-79 Schwartz (2002). For accuracy of psychic mentioned, see pp. 226-36.

PP. 180-81 Sogyal Rinpoche (1993).

P. 181 Tart (1990).

P. 181 Colin Wilson, see Wilson (1990).

P. 181 Opposing views of reincarnation and afterlife, see Edwards (1996).

P. 182 Atwater quote, Atwater (1994) p. 196.

P. 182 Sheldrake, see Sheldrake (2003) p. 81 and p. 285.

P. 183 Sharks detecting electric fields and quotation from Fields, see Fields (2007).

P. 184 Einstein spooky action at a distance, see Moring (2002) p. 270.

P. 184 Einhorn quotation, see Einhorn (2002) p. 165.

P. 185 Doore (1990).

P. 185 James quote, see http://whatthebleep.com/quotes/.

P. 185 Siegel quote, see Siegel (1989) p. 254.

## Chapter 11

P. 186  Emmet Fox quotation, see Siegel (1986) p. 205. Emmet Fox (1886-1951) was the minister of New York City's Church of the Healing.

# Bibliography

Ackerman, Diane, *An Alchemy of Mind: The Marvel and Mystery of the Brain*, New York, 2004, Scribner.

Ahlberg, Erik, and Clack, Jenneifer A., "A Firm Step from Water to Land," *Nature*, Vol. 440, 2006, pp. 747-9.

Al-Khalili, Jim, *Quantum*, London UK, 2003, Weidenfeld & Nicolson.

Alon, U., "Biological Networks: The Tinkerer as an Engineer," *Science*, Vol. 301, 2003, p. 1866.

Allwood, Abigail C., Walter, Malcolm R., Kamber, Balz S., Marshall, Craig P., and Burch, Ian W., "Stromatolite Reef from the Early Archaean Era of Australia," *Nature*, Vol 441, 2006, pp. 714-18.

Atwater, P. M. H., *Beyond the Light: What Isn't Being Said About Near-death Experience*, Secaucus, NJ, 1994, Birch Lane Press Book, Carol Publishing Group.

Baeckhed, Fredrik, Ley, Ruth E., Sonnenburg, Justin L.,Peterson, Daniel A., and Gordon, Jeffrey I., "Host-bacterial Mutualism in the Human Intestine," *Science*, Vol. 307, 2005, pp.1915-20.

Ball, Phillip, "Setting our Watches by Entanglement," *Nature*, Vol. 431, 2004, p. 756.

Barbour, Julian, *The End of Time: The Next Revolution in Physics*, New York, 1999, Oxford University Press.

Barsky, Arthur J., et al. "Nonspecific Medication Side Effects and the Nocebo

Phenomenon," *Journal of the American Medical Association*, Vol. 287, No. 5, February 6, 2002.

Bartusiak, Marcia, "Going the Distance," *Origin and Fate of the Universe, Astronomy*, special edition, 2004, pp. 64-71.

Becker, Robert O., and Selden, Gary, *The Body Electric: Electromagnetism and the Foundation of Life*, New York, 1985, Quill, William Morrow.

Becker, Robert O., *Cross Currents: The Promise of Electromedicine, the Perils of Electropollution*, New York, 1990, Jeremy P. Tarcher, Putnam, a member of Penguin Putnam Inc.

Benton, M. J, Tverdokhlebov, V. P., Surkov, M. V., "Ecosystems Remodeling Among Vertebrates at the Permian-triassic Boundry in Russia," *Nature*, Vol. 432, 2004, pp. 97-100.

Beukes, Nicolas, "Early Options in Photosynthesis," *Nature*, Vol. 431, 2004, pp. 522-3.

Blackmore, Susan, "Near-death Expiences: in or out of the Body?" *Skeptical Inquirer*, Vol. 16, 1991, pp. 34-45.

Bloom, Howard, *Global Brain: The Evolution of Mass Mind from the Big Bang to the 21ˢᵗ century*, New York, 2000, John Wiley & Sons, Inc.

Brack, André, editor, *The Molecular Origins of Life: Assembling Pieces of the Puzzle*, New York, 1998, Cambridge University Press.

Brand, Paul, and Yancey, Phillip, *Fearfully and Wonderfully Made: A Surgeon Looks at the Human and Spiritual Body*, Grand Rapids, MI, 1980, Zondervan Publishing House.

Bray, Dennis, "Molecular Networks: the Top-down View," *Science*, Vol. 301, 2003, p. 1864.

Bray, Dennis, *Cell Movements: From Molecules to Motility*, New York, 2001, Garland Publishing.

Briggs, D. E. G., Erwin, D. H., and Collier, F. J., *The Fossils of the Burgess Shale*, Washington, DC, 1994, Smithsonian Institute Press.

Brinkley, Dannion, *Saved by the Light: The True Story of a Man Who Died Twice and the Profound Revelations he Received*, New York, 1994, Villard Books.

Buchcanan, Mark, *Nexus: Small Worlds and the Groundbreaking Science of Networks*, New York, 2002, W. W. Norton and Company.

Brumfiel, Geoff, "In Search of Hidden Dimensions," *Nature*, Vol. 433, 2005, p. 10.

Campbell, Joseph, *Transformations of Myth Through Time*, New York, 1990, Harper & Row, Publishers.

Canfield, Don E., "Gas with an Ancient History," *Nature*, Vol. 440, 2006, pp. 426-7

Carter, Rita, *Exploring Consciousness*, Berkeley, CA, 2002, University of California Press.

Chopra, Deepak, *Quantum Healing: Exploring the Frontiers of Mind/Body Medicine*, New York, 1989, Bantum Books.

Clegg, Brian, *The God Effect: Quantum Entanglement, Science's Strangest Phenomenon*, New York, 2006, St. Martin's Press.

Crick, Francis, *Life Itself*, New York, 1981, Simon and Schuster.

Crick, Francis, *The Astonishing Hypothesis: The Scientific Search for the Soul*, New York, 1994, a Touchstone Book.

Cronin, John R., "Clues from the Origin of the Solar System: Meteorites," André Brack, editor, *The Molecular Origins of Life: Assembling the pieces of the puzzle*, Cambridge, UK, 1998, Cambridge University Press, pp. 119-146.

Daeschler, Edward B., Shubin, Neil H., and Jenkins, Farish A. Jr., "A devonian Tetrapod-like Fish and the Evolution of the Tetrapod Body Plan," *Nature*, Vol. 440, 2006, pp. 757-63.

De Duve, Christian, "The Onset of Selection," *Nature*, Vol. 433, 2005, pp. 581-2.

Deutsch, David, *The Fabric of Reality: The Science of Parallel Universes and its Implications*, New York, Allan Lane, 1997, Addison-Wesley.

Dobson, Christopher M., "Chemical Space and Biology," *Science*, Vol. 432, 2004, pp. 824-8.

Doidge, Norman, *The Brain That Changes Itself: Stories of Personal Triumph from the Frontiers of Brain Science*, New York, 2007, Viking.

Doore, Gary, editor, *What Survives? Contemporary Explorations of Life After Death*, edited by Gary Doore, Los Angeles, 1990, Jeremy P. Tarcher, Inc.

Dossey, Larry, *Recovering the Soul: A Scientific and Spiritual Search*, New York, 1989, Bantan Books.

Dossey, Larry, *Prayer is Good Medicine: How to Reap the Healing Benefits of Prayer*, New York, 1996, HarperSanFrancisco.

Dowling, John E., *The Great Brain Debate: Nature or Nurture?* Washington, DC, 2004, Joseph Henry Press.

Dvali, Gai, "Neutrino Probes of Dark Matter," *Science*, Vol. 300, 2004, pp. 567-8.

Dvali, G., "Out of Darkness," *Scientific American*, Vol. 290, 2004, pp. 68-75.

Dyson, Freeman, "The Darwinian Interlude-Biotechnology will Do Away with Species. Good: Cultural Evolution is Better Than Natural Selection," *Technology Reviews*, March 2005, p. 27.

Edwards, Paul, *Reincarnation: A Critical Examination*, New York, 1996, Prometheus Books.

Eid, Mounib El, "The Process of Carbon Creation," *Nature*, Vol. 433, 2005, pp 117-119.

Einhorn, Stefan, *A Concealed God: Religion, Science, and the Search for Truth*, Philadelphia, 2002, Templeton Foundation Press.

Erickson, Milton H., *The Collected Papers of Milton H. Erickson on Hypnosis: The nature of hypnosis and suggestion*, Vol. 2, New York, 1980, Irvington Publishers, Inc.

Feitelson, Jerry S., Payne, Jewel, and Kim, Leo, "Bacillus Thuringensis: Insects and Beyond," *Biotechnology*, Vol. 10, 1992, pp. 271-75.

Feitelson, Jerry S., "The Bacillus Thuringensis Family Tree," Leo Kim, editor, *Advanced Engineered Pesticides*, New York, 1993, Marcel Dekker. pp. 63-72.

Ferguson, Kitty, *The Fire in the Equations: Science, Religion and the Search for God*, Philadelphia, 2004, Templeton Foundation Press.

Ferris, James P., "Catalyzed RNA Synthesis for the RNA World," André Brack, editor, *The Molecular Origins of Life: Assembling the Pieces of the Puzzle*, Cambridge, UK, 1998, Cambridge University Press.

Feynman, Richard P., Leighton, Robert B., and Sands, Matthew, *The Feynman Lectures on Physics: Mainly mechanical, radiation, and heat*, Vol. 1, Menlo Park, CA, 1963, Addison-Wesley Publishing Company.

Fields, R. Douglas, "Making Memories Stick," *Scientific American*, Vol. 292, February 2005, pp. 74-81.

Fields, R. Douglas, "The Shark's Electric Sense," *Scientific American*, Vol. 297, August, 2007, pp. 75-80.

Figer, Donald F., "An Upper Limit to the Masses of Stars," *Nature*, Vol. 434, 2005, pp. 192-4.

Filmore, David, "Cataloging Clinical Trials," *Modern Drug Discovery*, October 2004, pp. 39-41.

Fisk, M. R., Popu, R., Mason, O. U., Storrie-Lombardi, M. C., Vicenzi, E. P., "Iron-magnesium Silicate Bioweathering on Earth (and Mars?)" *Astrobiology*, Vol. 6, no. 1, Feb. 2006, pp. 48-68.

Fox, Matthew, and Sheldrake, Rupert, *Natural Grace: Dialogues on Creation, Darkness, and the Soul in Spirituality and Science*, New York, 1996, Doubleday.

Friedman, Norman, *Bridging Science and Spirit: Common Elements in David Bohm's physics, the Perennial Philosophy and Seth*, St. Louis, MO, 1990, Living Lakes Books.

Fritzsch, Harald, Translated by Karin Heusch, *The Curvature of Spacetime: Newton, Einstein, and Gravitation*, New York, 1996, Columbia University Press.

Fry, Iris, *The Emergence of Life on Earth: A Historical and Scientific Overview*, New Brunswick, NJ, 2000, Rutgers University Press.

Gale, Robert Peter, and Hauser, Thomas, *Chernobyl: The Final Warning*, London, 1988, Hamish Hamilton Ltd.

Gallup: *US Key Indicators*, January 2000, Gallup UK for BBC Soul or Britain.

Gallup, George, Jr., with William Proctor, *Adventures in Immortality*, New York, 1982, McGraw-Hill Book Company.

Gardner, James, *The Intelligent Universe: AI, ET, and the Emerging Mind of the Cosmos*, Franklin Lakes, NJ, 2007, New Page Books.

Gehrels, N., Piro, L., Leonard, P. J. T., "The Brightest Explosions in the Universe," The Secret Lives of Starts, *Scientific American*, special edition, Vol. 14, 2004, pp. 93-100.

Gleiser, Marcelo, "The Three Origins: Cosmos, Life, and Mind," *Science and Ultimate Reality: Quantum Theory, Cosmology, and Complexity*, Cambridge, UK, 2004, University Press, pp. 637-653.

Gott, J. Richard, *Time Travel in Einstein's Universe*, New York, 2001, Houghton Mifflin Company.

Greene, Brian, *The Fabric of the Cosmos*, New York, 2004, Alfred A. Knopf.

Griffith, C. A., et. al., "Evidence for a Polar Ethane Cloud on Titan," *Science*, Vol. 313, 2006, pp. 1620-22.

Guth, Alan H., and Kaiser, David I., "Inflationary Cosmology: Exploring the Universe from the Smallest to the Largest Scales," *Science*, Vol. 307, 2005, pp. 884-890.

Gyatso, Tenzin (His Holiness the Dalai Lama), *The Universe in a Single Atom: the Convergence of Science and Spirituality*, New York, 2005, Morgan Road Books.

Halpern, Paul, and Wesson, Paul, *Brave New Universe: Illuminating the Darkest Secrets of the Cosmos*, Washington, DC, 2006, Joseph Henry Press.

Hamer, Dean, *The God Gene: How Faith is Hardwired into our Genes*, New York, 2004, Doubleday.

Hameroff, Stuart, Chalmers, David John, Kaszniak, Alfred W., *Towards a Science of Consciousness III: the Third Tucson Discussions and Debates*, New York, 1999, Bradford Books.

Hanlon, R. T., Forsythe, J. W., and Joneschild, D. E., *Biol. J. Linn. Soc.*, Vol. 66 (1999) p. 1.

Henry, Richard Conn, "The Mental Universe," *Nature*, Vol. 436, 2005, p. 29.

Hofstadter, Douglas, *I Am A Strange Loop*, Cambridge MA, 2007, Basic Books.

Hooft, Gerard 't, Susskin, Leonard, Witten, Edward, Fukagita, Masataka, Randall, Lisa, Smolin, Lee, Stachel, John, Rovelli, Carlo, Ellis, George, Weinberg, Steven, and Penrose, Roger, "A Theory of Everything?" *Nature*, Vol. 433, 2005, pp. 257-259.

Hooper, Dan, *Dark Cosmos: In Search of our Universe's Missing Mass and Energy*, New York, 2006, HarperCollins Publishers.

Hoyle, Fred, and Wickramasinghe, Chandra, *Lifecloud*, New York, 1979, Harper and Row.

Hoyle, Fred, and Wickramasinghe, Chandra, *Disease from Space*, New York, 1979, Harper and Row.

Hunt, Valerie V., *Infinite Mind: Science of the Human Vibrations of Consciousness*, Malibu, CA, 1996, Malibu Publishing Co.

International Human Genome Sequencing Consortium, "Finishing the Euchromatic Sequence of the Human Genome," *Nature*, Vol. 431, 2004, p. 931-945.

Irion, Robert, "The Warped Side of Dark Matter," *Science*, Vol. 300, 2003, pp 1894-6.

James, Kenneth D., and Ellington, Andrew D., "Catalysis in the RNA world," André Brack, editor, *The Molecular Origins of Life-Assembling the Pieces of the Puzzle*, Cambridge, UK, 1998, Cambridge University Press, pp. 269-294.

Jasny, Barbara R., and Ray, L. Brian, "Life and the Art of Networks," *Science*, Vol. 301, 2003, p. 1863.

Kaku, Michio, *Parallel Worlds: A Journey Through Creation, Higher Dimensions, and the Future of the Cosmos*, New York, 2005, Doubleday.

Kandel, Eric R., Schwartz, James H., and Jessell, Thomas M., *Principles of Neural Science*, Third Edition, Norwalk, Connecticut, 1991, Appleton & Lange.

Kanipe, Jeff, *Chasing Hubble's Shadows: The Search for Galaxies at the Edge of Time*, New York, 2006, Hill and Wang.

Kaplan, Rob, editor, *Science Says*, New York, 2001, W. H. Freeman and Company.

Kauffman, Stuart, "Autonomous Agents," *Science and Ultimate Reality: Quantum Theory, Cosmology, and Complexity*, Cambridge, UK, 2004, University Press, pp. 654-666.

Kenyon, S. J., and Bromley, B. C., "Stellar Encounters as the Origin of Distant Solar System: Objects in Highly Eccentric Orbits," *Nature*, Vol., 432, 2004, pp. 598-602.

Kerr, Richard A., "Did Jupiter and Saturn Team Up to Pummel the Inner Solar System?" *Science*, Vol. 306, 2004, p. 1676.

Kerr, Richard A., "A Shot of Oxygen to Unleash the Evolution of Animals," *Science*, Vol. 314, 2006 p. 1529.

Kim, Leo, editor, *Advanced Engineered Pesticides*, New York, 1993, Marcel Dekker.

Kim, Leo, and Wald, M. M., "Conversion of Butadiene and Methanol" U.S. Patent 4,126,642 1978.

Kim, Leo, Wald, M. M., and Brandenberger, S. G., "One-step Catalytic Synthesis of 2,2,3-trimethylbutane from Methanol," *Journal of Organic Chemistry*, Vol. 43, 1978, pp. 3432-33.

Kirshner, R. P., "Throwing Light on Dark Energy," *Science*, Vol. 300, 2003, pp. 1914-18.

Klein, H. P., "On the Search for Extant Life on Mars," *Icarus*, Vol. 120, 1996, pp. 431-436.

Knoll, Andrew H., *Life on a Young Planet: the First Three Billion Years of Evolution on Earth*, Princeton, NJ, 2003, Princeton University Press.

Krasner, Robert I., *The Microbial Challenge: Human-microbe Interactions*, Washington, DC, 2002, ASM Press.

Krauss, Lawrence M., "What is Dark Energy?" *Nature*, Vol. 431, 2004, p. 519.

Kwok, Sun, "The Synthesis of Organic and Inorganic Compounds in Evolved Stars," *Nature*, Vol. 430, 2004, p. 985.

Land, Edwin H., "The Retinex Theory of Color Vision," *Scientific American*, December 1977, pp. 108-128.

Land, Edwin H., "Experiments in Color Vision," *Scientific American*, May 1959, no. 5.

Lane, Nick, *Power, Sex, Suicide: Mitochondria and the Meaning of Life*, New York, 2005, Oxford University Press.

Lane, Nick, "Reading the Book of Death," *Nature*, Vol. 448, July 12, 2007, pp. 1222-125

Larson, R. B., and Bloom, V., "The First Stars in the Universe," The Secret Lives of Stars, *Scientific American*, Special edition, Vol.14, 2004 pp.4-11.

Laughlin, Robert B., *A Different Universe: Reinventing Physics from the Bottom Down*, New York, 2005, Basic Books.

Lax, Eric, *Life and Death on 10 West*, New York, 1984, Dell Publishing Co., Inc.

Lazar, Sara W., Kerr, Catherine E., Wasserman, Rachel H., Gray, Jeremy R., Greve, Douglas N., Treadway, Michael T., McGarvey, Metta, Quinn, Brain T., Dusek, Jeffery A., Benson, Herbert, Rauch, Scott L., Moore, Christorpher I., and Fischl, Bruce, "Meditation Experiences is Associated with Increased Cortical Thickness," *NeuroReport*, Nov. 28, 2005 pp. 1893-97.

Lee, Der-Chaun, Halliday, A. H., Snyder, G. A., and Taylor, L. A., "Age and Origin of the Moon," *Science*, Vol. 278, 1997, pp. 1098-1103.

Leroi, Armand Marie, *Mutants: On the Form, Varieties & Errors of the Human Body*, London, 2003, Harper Collins Publishers.

Lewin, Benjamin, *Genes VI*, New York, 1997, Oxford University Press.

Lewin, Roger, *Making Waves: Irving Dardik and his Superwave Principle*, USA, 2005, Rodale.

Lineweaver, Charles H., and Davis, Tamara M., "Misconceptions About the Big Bang," *Scientific American*, March, 2005, pp. 36-45.

Livio, Mario, "Moving Right Along: The Accelerating Universe Holds Clues to Dark Energy, the Big Bang, and the Ultimate Beauty of Nature," *Origin and Fate of the Universe, Astronomy*, special cosmology issue, 2004. pp 94-99.

Lloyd, Seth, and Ng, Y. Jack, "Black Hole Computer," *Scientific American*, Vol. 291, 2004, p. 53.

Lloyd, Seth, *Programming the Universe: A Quantum Computer Scientist Takes on the Cosmos*, New York, 2006, Alfred A. Knof.

McKay, Christopher P., "Life on Mars," André Brack, editor, *The Molecular Origins of Life: Assembling the Pieces of the Puzzle*, Cambridge, UK, 1998, Cambridge University Press, p. 386-406.

McKay, Christopher P., Gibson, E. K., Thompas-Keprta, K. L., Vail, H., Romanek, C. S., Clement, S. J., Chiller, X. D., Maechling, C.R., and Zare, R. N., "Search for Past Life on Mars: Possible Relic Biogenic Activity in Martian Meteorite ALH84001," *Science*, Vol., 273, 1996, pp. 924-930.

Margulis, Lynn, and Sagan, Dorion, *Microcosmos: Four Billion Years of Microbial Evolution*, New York, 1986, Summit Books.

Maurette, Micheal, "Micrometeorites on the Early Earth," André Brack, editor, *The Molecular Origins of Life: Assembling the Pieces of the Puzzle*, Cambridge, UK, 1998, Cambridge University Press, pp. 147-186.

Miller, Ronald S., and the Editors of New Age Journal, *As Above So Below: Paths to Spiritual Renewal in Daily Life*, Los Angeles, 1992, Jeremy P. Tarcher, Inc.

Miralda-Escude, Jordi, "The Dark Age of the Universe," *Science*, Vol. 300, 2003, pp. 1904-9.

Mithen, Steven, *The Prehistory of the Mind: The Cognitive Origins of Art, Religion, and Science*, New York, 1996, Thames and Hudson.

Moorbath, Stephen, "Dating Earliest Life," *Nature*, Vol. 434, 2005, p. 155.

Moring, Gary F., *The Complete Idiot's Guide to the Theories of the Universe*, Indianapolis, IN, 2002, Alpha, a Pearson Education Company.

Nadis, Steve, "Will Dark Energy Steal the Stars?" *Origin and Fate of the Universe, Astronomy*, special edition, 2004, pp. 100-105.
Nealson, K. H., "The Limits of Life on Earth and Searching for Life on Mars," *J. Geophys. Res.*, Vol. 102, 1997, pp. 23675-23686.

Newberg, Andrew, D'Aquili, Eugene, and Rause, Vince, *Why God Won't Go Away: Brain Science and the Biology of Belief*, New York, 2001, Ballantine Books.

Noble, Elizabeth, with Leo Sorger, *Having Twins and More: A parent's Guide to Multiple Pregnancy, Birth and Early Childhood*, New York, 2003, Houghton Mifflin Company.

Orgel, Leslie E., "RNA Catalysis and the Origin of Life," *Journal of Theoretical Biology*, Vol. 123, 1986, pp. 12-149.

Orgel, Leslie E., "The Origin of Biological Information", *Life's Origin: the Beginning of Biological Evolution*, edited by J. William Schopf, Berkeley CA, 2002, University of California Press, pp. 140-157.

Ornish, Dean, *Love and Survival: 8 Pathways to Intimacy and Health*, New York, 1998, HarperCollins.

Ornstein, Robert, *The Roots of the Self: Unraveling the Mystery of Who We Are*, New York, 1993, Harper San Francisco, HarperCollins Publishers.

Ornstein, Robert, *Multimind*, Boston, 1986, Houghton Mifflin.

Ornstein, Robert, *Evolution of Consciousness: The Origins of the Way We Think*, New York, 1991, Simon & Schuster.

Ornstein, Robert, *The Right Mind*, New York, 1997, Harcourt Brace & Company

Oro, John, "Historical Understanding of Life's Beginnings," J. William Schopf, editor, *Life's Origin: The Beginning of Biological Evolution*, Los Angeles, 2002, University of California Press.

Ostriker, J. P. and Steinhardt, P., "New Light on Dark Matter," *Science*, Vol. 300, 2003, pp. 1909-13.

Ostriker, J. P. and Steinhardt, P., "The Quintessential Universe," *Scientific American*, Vol. 284, 2001, pp. 46-53.

Parker, Andrew, *In the Blink of an Eye*, Cambridge, MA, 2003, Perseus Books Group.

Pennisi, Elizabeth, "A Mouthful of Microbes," *Science*, Vol. 307, 2005, pp. 1899-1901.

Pennisi, Elizabeth, "A Genomic View of Animal Behavior," *Science*, Vol. 307, 2005, pp. 30-32.

Penrose, Roger, *The Road to Reality: A Complete Guide to the Laws of the Universe*, New York, 2004, Alfred A. Knopf.

Pert, Candice, *Molecules of Emotion*, New York, 1999, Simon and Schuster.

Pert, Candice, "Why do We Feel the Way We Feel?" *The Seer*, December 3, 2002.

Radin, Dean I., *The Conscious Universe: The Scientific Truth of Psychic Phenomena*, New York, 1997, HarperSanFrancisco.

Rees, Martin, *Before the Beginning: Our Universe and Others*, Reading, MA, 1997, Helix Books, Addison-Wesley.

Rescher, Nicholas, *G. W. Leibniz's Monadology: An Edition for Students*, Pittsburg, PA, 1991, University of Pittsburg Press.

Restak, Richard, *The New Brain: How the Modern Age is Rewiring your Mind*, USA, 2004, Holtzbrinck Publishers.

Ridley, Matt, *The Agile Gene: How Nature Turns on Nurture*, New York, 2004, HarperCollins Publishers.

Rinpoche, Sogyal, *The Tibetan Book of the Living and Dying*, New York, 1993, Harper San Francisco.

Riordan, Michael, and Zajc, William A., "The First Few Seconds," *Scientific American*, May, 2006, pp. 34-41.

Rossi, Ernest, *The Psychobiology of Mind: Body Healing-New Concepts of Therapeutic Hypnosis*, New York, 1986, W. W. Norton & Company.

Rowan, Linda, and Coontz, Robert, "Welcome to the Dark Side: Delighted to See You," *Science*, Vol. 300, 2003, p. 1893.

Sabom, Micheal, *Light and Death: One Doctor's Account of Near-death Experiences*, Grand Rapids, MI, 1998, Zondervan Publishing House.

Sabom, Micheal, "'The Shadow of Death," *Christian Research Journal*, Vol. 26, no. 2, 2003.

Sacks, Oliver, *The Island of the Colorblind and Cycad Island*, New York, 1997, Alfred A. Knopf..

Sagan, Carl, *Cosmos*, New York, 1980, Random House.

Sagan, Carl, *Broca's Brain: Reflections on the Romance of Science*, Canada, 1974, Random House.

Satinover, Jeffrey, *The Quantum Brain: The Search for Freedom and the Next Generation of Man*, New York, 2001, John Wiley and Sons, Inc.

Savile, Anthony, *Leibniz and the Monadology*, New York, 2000, Routledge.

Schilling, Sovert, "String Revival," *Scientific American*, February 2005, p. 25.

Schopf, J. William, "Tracing the Roots of the Universal Tree of Life," André Brack, editor, *The Molecular Origins of Life: Assembling the Pieces of the Puzzle*, Cambridge, UK, 1998, Cambridge University Press, pp. 336-362.

Schopf, J. William, "The What, When, and How of Life's Beginnings," J. William Schopf, editor, *Life's Origin: The Beginning of Biological Evolution*,

Los Angeles, 2002, University of California Press.

Schwartz, Gary E., *The Afterlife Experiments: Breakthrough Scientific Evidence of Life After Death*, New York, 2002, Pocket Books.

Schwartz, Gary E. R., and Russek, Linda, G. S., *The Living Energy Universe: A Fundamental Discovery that Transforms Science and Medicine*, Charlottesvill, VA, 1999, Hampton Roads Publishing Co., Inc.

Schwartz, Jeffrey M., and Begley, Sharon, *The Mind and the Brain: Neuroplasticity and the Power of Mental Force*, New York, 2002, Regan Books.

Searle, John R., *Mind: A Brief Introduction*, New York, 2004, Oxford University Press.

Segal, Alan F., *Life After Death: A History of the Afterlife in the Religions of the West*, New York, 2004, Doubleday.

Seife, Charles, *Alpha & Omega: the Search for the Beginning and End of the Universe*, New York, 2003, Penguin Books.

Seife, Charles, "Dark Energies Tiptoes towards the Spotlight," *Science*, Vol. 300, 2003, pp.1896-7.

Seife, Charles, "Physics Enters the Twilight Zone," *Science*, Vol. 305, 2004, pp. 464-6.

Sheldrake, Rupert, *The Sense of Being Stared At: and Other Aspects of the Extended Mind*, New York, 2003, Crown Publishers.

Shubin, Neil H., Daeschler, Edward B., and Jenkins, Farish A. Jr., "The Pectoral Fin of Tiktaalik Roseae and the Origin of the Tetrapod Limb," *Nature*, Vol. 440, 2006, pp. 764-771.

Siegel, Bernie S., *Love, Medicine & Miracles: Lessons Learned About Self-healing from a Surgeon's Experience with Exceptional Patients*, New York, 1986, Harper & Row.

Siegel, Bernie S., *Peace, Love & Healing*, New York, 1989, Quill, an imprint of HaperCollins Publishers.

Smolin, Lee, *Three Roads to Quantum Gravity*, New York, 2001, Basic Books, Perseus Books Group, 2001.

Sneden, C., and Cowan, J., "Genesis of the Heaviest Elements in the Milky Way Galaxy," *Science*, Vol. 299, 2003, pp. 70-5.

Soloman, Sean C., et al, "New Perspectives on Ancient Mars," *Science*, Vol. 307, 2005, pp.1214-19.

Spiney, Laura, "Anarchy in the hive," *New Scientist*, January 15, 2005, pp. 42-45.

Stewart, Matthew, *The Courtier and the Heretic: Leibniz, Spinoza, and the Fate of God in the Modern World*, New York, 2006, W. W. Norton & Company.

Straus, Eugene W., and Straus, Alex, *Medical Marvels: The 100 Greatest Advances in Medicine*, New York, 2006, Prometheus Books.

Talbot, Michael, *The Holographic Universe*, New York, 1991, HarperCollins Publishers.

Tanaka, Kozo, et al, "Molecular Mechanisms of Kinetochore Capture by Spindle Microtubules," *Nature*, Vol. 434, 2005, pp. 987-94.

Targ, Russel, and Katra, Jane, *Miracles of Mind: Exploring Nonlocal Consciousness and Spiritual Healing*, Novato, CA, 1998, New World Library.

Tart, Charles T., *What Survives? Contemporty Exploration of Life After Death*, edited by Gary Doore, Los Angeles, 1990, Jeremy P. Tarcher, Inc.

Tauber, Daniel I., "The Quest for Holism in Medicine," *The Role of Complementary & Alternative Medicine*, Daniel Callahan, editor, Washington, D.C., 2002, Georgetown University Press, pp. 172-189.

Tegmark, Max, "Parallel Universes-not just a Staple of Science Fiction: Other Universes are a Direct Implication of Cosmological Observations," *Scientific American special report Parallel Universes*, 2005, pp. 1-13.

Tegmark, Max, "Parallel Universes," *Science and Ultimate Reality: Quantum Theory, Cosmology, and Complexity*, Edited by John D. Barrow, Paul W. Davis, and Charles L. Harper, Jr., Cambridge, UK, 2004, Cambridge University press, pp. 459-491.
Tice, Michael M., and Lowe, Donald R., "Photosynthetic Microbial Mats in the 3,416 Million Year Old Ocean," *Nature*, Vol. 431, 2004, pp549-52.

Tiller, William A., *Science and Human Transformation: Subtle Energies, Intentionality and Consciousness*, Walnut Creek, CA, 1997, Pavior Publishing
.

Tolson, Chester L, and Koenig, Harold G., *The Healing Power of Prayer*, Grand Rapids, MI, 2003, Baker Books.

Tyson, Neil deGrasse, and Goldsmith, Donald, *Origins: Fourteen Billion Years of Cosmic Evolution*, New York, 2004, W. W. Norton & Company

Ueno, Yuichiro, Yamada, Keita, Yoshida, Naohiro, Maruyama, Shigenori, and Isozaki, Yukio, "Evidence from Fluid Inclusions for Microbial Methanogenesis in Early Achaean Era," *Nature*, Vol. 440, 2006, pp. 516-19.

Valley, John W., "A Cool Early Earth?" *Scientific American*, October 2005, pp. 59-65.

Van Lommel, Pim, van Wess, Ruud, Meyers, Vincent, and Elfferich, Ingrid, "Near-death Experiences in Survivors of Cardiac Arrest: a Prospective Study in the Netherlands," *The Lancet*, December 15, 2001, pp.2039-2045.

Vedral, Vlatko, "Entanglement Hits the Big Time," *Nature*, 425, pp. 28-9, 2003.

Wald, M. M., and Kim, Leo, "Process for Producing Triptane by Contacting Methanol or Dimethyl Ether with Zinc Chloride," U.S. Patent 4,059,647 1977.

Wald, M. M., and Kim, Leo, "Process for Producing Triptane by Contacting Methanol or Dimethyl Ether with Zinc Bromide," U.S. Patent 4,059,646 1977.

Watts, Duncan J., *Six Degrees: The Science of a Connected age*, New York, 2003, London, W. W. Norton & Company.

Webb, Stephen, *Out of this World: Colliding Universe, Branes, Strings, and Other Wild Ideas of Modern Physics*, New York, 2004, Copernicus Books.

*Webster's New World Dictionary of Quotations*, Hoboken, NJ, 2005, Wiley Publishing, Inc.

Wilczek, Frank, *Fantastic Realities: 49 Mind Journeys and a Trip to Stockholm*, New Jersey, 2006, World Scientific.

Wilson, Colin, *What Survives?: Contemporary Explorations of Life After Death*, edited by Gary Doore, Los Angeles, 1990, Jeremy P. Tarcher, Inc.

Witham, Larry, *The Measure of God: Our Century-Long Struggle to Reconcile Science and Religion*, New York, 2005, HarperSanFrancisco.

Witten, Edward, "Universe on a String," *Origin and Fate of the Universe, Astronomy*, special edition, 2004, pp. 42-47.

Wolfram, Steven, *A New Kind of Science*, Champaign, IL, 2002, Wolfram Media, Inc.

Wong, Kate, "The Morning of the Modern Mind," *Scientific American*, June 2005, pp. 86-95.

Zatorre, Robert, Music, "The Food of Neurosciences," *Nature*, Vol. 434, 2005, pp. 312-315.

Zeilinger, Anton, Editors: John D. Barrow, Paul C. W. Davies, and Charles L. Harper, Jr., "Why the Quantum?, *Science and Ultimate Reality: Quantum Theory, Cosmology, and Complexity*, Cambridge, UK, 2004, University Press, pp. 201-220.

Zhao, Min et al, "Electrical Signals Control Wound Healing Through Phosphatidylinositol-3-OH Kinase Gamma and PTEN" *Nature*, Vol. 442, 2006, pp. 457-60.

Zimmer, Carl, *Discover*, February, 2005, pp. 29-35.

# Index

Feynman, Richard 62-63

Fields, R. Douglas 183

Fox, Emmet 186

Fox, Matthew 1, 3, 31, 152

Franciscan nuns 138, 140

Free will 122, 126-28, 189

Fry, Iris 31

# G

Gale, Robert Peter (Bob) 2, 18-20

Gallup, George Jr. 140, 142, 169

Gardner, Rex 141

God: A Concealed God, 184; beliefs
  about. See under Religion; consciousness, and, 118; dualism, and
  117; in NDEs, 170; is incomprehensible, 150-51 (see Gregory of Nyssa);
  mental apparatus, (see Dyson,
  Freeman); monotheism, 152 (see
  Christianity); multiple gods, 152 (see
  Religions); prayer, and, 139, reality,
  and 150-51; spirituality, and. See
  under Spirituality; The God Effect,
  86; Why God Won't Go Away, 138

Gospel of Thomas 150

Gram-positive bacteria 18, 44

Greene, Brian 83

Gregory of Nyssa 149

Guth, Alan 59-60

# H

Haldane, J.B.S. 76

Hamer, Dean 101

Hameroff, Stuart 176, 184

Hawking, Stephen 9, 64

Healing Mind, the 129-45; hypnosis, 131-34; power of, 144-45; (see
  also Meditation, Nocebo effect,
  Placebo effect, Prayer)

Heaven 83, 166-67

Henry, Richard 55, 69, 160

Heisenberg, Werner 163

Higgs field 7, 12

Hinduism 151-52, 167

Hindus 68, 161

Hoyle, Sir Fred 21, 24, 29

Human energy field 154-55, 157

Hunt, Valerie 154-55, 157, 182

# I

Indian. See eastern religions

Inflation: description and timing of,
  5-6; odds of, 8-10, 16-17, 29-30

Intelligent design 4

Islam 151-52

# J

James, William 185

Jeans, Sir James Hopwood 128, 159

Jesus 140, 150

Josephson, Brian 86

Judaism 151-52, 167

Jung, Carl G. 121, 144-45

# K

Kabbalah 153

attempts at (see Jeans, Sir James
Hopewood; Ward, Keith); photons,
and, 63-64; plastic brain, and, 123;
process philosophy, and, 116; relativity theory, and, 67; technology, and,
63; the 20th century, and, 74, 159;
the immaterial, 160

# R

Rause, Vince 138
Realms of reality 70-71, 73, 120-21, 171
Rees, Sir Martin 9, 58
Reiki 153
Reincarnation 166-67, 180
Religion: beliefs about God, and, 152;
love, and, 162-63; metaphors, 141,
151; science, and, 4; the spiritual,
and, 114
Religions: Azetec, 154; Bantu, 154;
Mayan 151, 154; Mesoamerican,
154; Mixtec, 154; Native American
154; traditional African, 154; (see
also Australian Aboriginals, Bud-
dhism, Christianity, Confucianism,
Eastern religions, Hinusidm, Islam,
Judaism, Taoist, and, Vedic teach-
ings)
Reynolds, Pam 175-76
Restak, Richard 122
Rinpoche, Sogyal 180
Rossi, Ernest Lawrence 129-30

# S

Sabom, Michael 174
Sagan, Carl i, 17, 178
Saroyan, William 145
Satinover, Jeffrey 62, 124
Schoff, J. William 30
Schwartz, Jeffrey 116-17, 122-23, 125
Seife, Charles 12
Sheldrake, Rupert 177, 182, 184
Siegel, Bernie 142, 177, 184-85
Space-time 62, 83, 85
Spetzler, Robert 175
Spinoza, Benedict de 165
Spirit: after death (see Doore, Gary;
Tibetan Book of the Dead); as a
"vital principle" or life giving, 152;
clues to the afterlife, and, 167;
explanation and metaphors of, (see
Fox, Matthew); healed by love, 190;
Polynesian belief in energy, 153; science, and, 151; superior, 91
Spiritual: awakening 3, 185, 190; consciousness, 117; embrace of the
spiritual by scientists, 163; energy,
153; essence and information realm,
181; explanations of NDEs, 173-74;
healer, Jane Katra (see Katra, Jane);
healing, 188; healing and love, 142;
human brain, 106; ideal monist
belief, 118; individuals and the concept of reality, 159; knowledge, 188;
leaders and truth, 187; meditation,

consciousness, 121, 127, 157-58; molecules, and, 110; movement causes mass, 82; oneness, and, 142; play musical chairs, 62-63; quantum theory, and, 152; realms of reality, and. See Realms of reality; survive our death, 183, 188-89; telepathy, and, 67; time, and, 87; transforms into elements, 8; understanding creation, and, 51; unknown history of, 187; vacuum states, and, 59; wholeness, and, 67, 91; zip in and out of our world, 72, 187

## V

van Lommel, Pim 172-74
Vedic teachings 137, 153
Vedral, Vlatko 86

## W

Ward, Keith 163
Webb, Stephen 70
Weinberg, Steven 84-85, 171
Wheeler, John 17, 33, 51, 62-65
Whitehead, Alfred 116-17, 151
Wickramasinghe, Chandra 29
Wigner, Eugene 126
Wilczek, Frank 58
Wilson, Colin 181

## Z

Zatorre, Robert 106